OPEN
KITCHEN

OPEN
KITCHEN

A Chef's Day
at
The Inn at Bay Fortune

BY MICHAEL SMITH

Callawind
Publications Inc.

MONTREAL

Open Kitchen: A Chef's Day at The Inn at Bay Fortune

CATALOGUING IN PUBLICATION DATA

Smith, Michael, 1966–
    Open kitchen : a chef's day at The Inn at Bay Fortune

Includes index.
ISBN 1-896511-10-4

    1. Cookery—Prince Edward Island—Bay Fortune.
2. Inn at Bay Fortune. I. Title.

TX649.S55A3 1998   641.5'09717'7   C98-900479-1

Book design by Shari Blaukopf. Copy editing by Sarah Weber. Indexing by Christine Jacobs. Illustrations by Michael Smith.
Front cover photo of Spice Rubbed Tuna Loin with Saffron Ratatouille, Tomato Anchovy Sauce, and Swiss Chard by Julian Beverage.
Front cover photo of Michael Smith by Jack Leclair.

10 9 8 7 6 5 4 3 2 1

Printed in Canada. All product/brand names are trademarks or registered trademarks of their respective trademark holders.

Published by Callawind Publications Inc., 3383 Sources Boulevard, Suite 205, Dollard-des-Ormeaux, Quebec, Canada H9B 1Z8 / 2083 Hempstead Turnpike, Suite 355, East Meadow, New York, USA 11554-1730; http://www.callawind.com.
Distributed in North America by Firefly Books Ltd., 3680 Victoria Park Avenue, Willowdale, Ontario, Canada M2H 3K1.

CONTENTS

Evening

FOREWORD

The philosophy of culinary regionalism, the one you will encounter in *Open Kitchen,* is not new. It's the way the French, the Spanish, the Italians, the Chinese, indeed, all ancient cultures, have always approached their tables. In the lands of these cultures, it is common to find foods so specific that a valley or two away they are unknown or, at the very least, unused.

Here in Canada, the same thing has existed since the First Peoples traded camas lily roots for eulachon grease. But it was not until recently that Canadians, primarily chefs, have recognized Canadian cuisine. Before, it was an oxymoron. Today, it is dynamic, revolutionary, ultimately regional, and filled to overflowing with fabulous new tastes.

As a food writer, my own culinary journey began in 1982 exploring the farmers markets of my home province, Ontario. It was a magnificent experience talking to vendors about the products they grew and collecting their favourite recipes. But where else could such immediacy be found? The answer . . . at country inns!

In the ensuing years, I've searched, sampled, and marvelled at the diversity of the foods of this nation served in the dining rooms of dozens of top flight, dare I say world class, establishments. There is no question that The Inn at Bay Fortune is one of the very finest. There energy flows, creativity is nurtured, beauty is honoured. Chef Michael Smith and master innkeeper/dream-meister David Wilmer really get it.

Michael Smith is a purist . . . the closer to home it's grown, the greater the chance you'll find it on one of his menus. It's difficult to say whether the tall, blue-eyed chef is happier at his stoves, on a fishing boat helping to haul in lobster traps, or poking about the great little farmers market in Charlottetown. From the fabulous blue mussels flourishing in the Murray River estuary just down the road to the wild mint that Smith gleefully found growing nearby several summers ago, the finest of island ingredients are reflected in the menus at the Inn and in this book, which will provide you with an honest glimpse of the new Canadian cuisine.

So if, on some sunny, cerulean-blue, Prince Edward Island summer's day, you want a meal of a lifetime, pack your bags and head for The Inn at Bay Fortune, or open this book and escape into the great aromas and flavours of Michael Smith's *Open Kitchen.*

— **Anita Stewart**
Culinary activist/author

ACKNOWLEDGMENTS

This tale is dedicated to the people who have inspired my cooking, a metaphor for my life. Cheers to you all!

* My family: my mom, my dad, and my brothers Philip and Stephen. Thanks for enduring my food before I knew what cooking was. Susannah, Kathleen, and Hubert, welcome! I love you all!
* My friends: the Espenhorsts, who've seen it all; Dave, my wave and wind sensei; Mike, Florida's best; Pierce, the Texas cowboy; Bob, the California dreamer; Christine, the L.A. hotshot; Rolf, another North Atlantic fanatic; Pat; Tony; and Joerg, Stefan, Hans, and my other island mates, Louise, Gretha, Paul, Greg, the brothers, my sailing buddies, and the ladies.
* The chefs: Paul Sartory, my mentor; Brett, the first; Joe, little did he know; the Culinary Institute of America instructors; and Larry, David, and Michel.
* The cooks: my grandmother, for her cornbread; Dot, who taught me gracious hospitality; Flossie, who can start a party anywhere; Mr. Jennings; and the folks who make those perfect, fresh bite-size doughnuts at the farmers market!
* Team Cuisine: sous-chef Jeff McCourt, the guts of the operation; first cook Norman, the natural; Jennifer, the life of the kitchen party; Lance, the up and comer; Brent; Gord; Andrew; Jeff; Craig; Greg; everyone else who has ever cooked at the Inn; and most of all, our dishwashers!
* My Inn family, friends, and teammates (together we made The Inn at Bay Fortune what it is today):

Anne and Ned Wilmer, our collective grandparents; Bonnie, Carol, Audrey, Linda, Wendy, Sharon, Lisa, Loretta, and everyone who has contributed to the hospitality of our dining room; Debbie, Suzie (happy birthday!), Stacy, and their partners-in-crime; Carol; Phil, our philosopher; Clarice and Fulton, the creators of our kitchen garden; and the guy who never stops cutting the lawn.
* The farmers, fishers, and culinary community of Prince Edward Island: Edwin, the local yachtsman; Steve, the baker, for his colorful flours; Rundell, the gingerman; the Culinary Institute of Canada; Carol; Denise; June-Ellen; Peter; Paul; Brad; Brett; Joe and Gale; the gang at the farmers market; and whoever grows potatoes for McDonalds.
* The artists who contributed to this book: Jack, a magician with his action camera; Julian, the stylish close-up artist; Anita, a true inspiration to all who love Canada; and the design and production team.
* David Wilmer, friend, teacher, mentor, innkeeper, business partner, food critic, and struggling windsurfer. Thanks for your vision and tenacity. We're just getting started.
* The guests, past and future, that inspire us.

WELCOME

A Chef's Journey

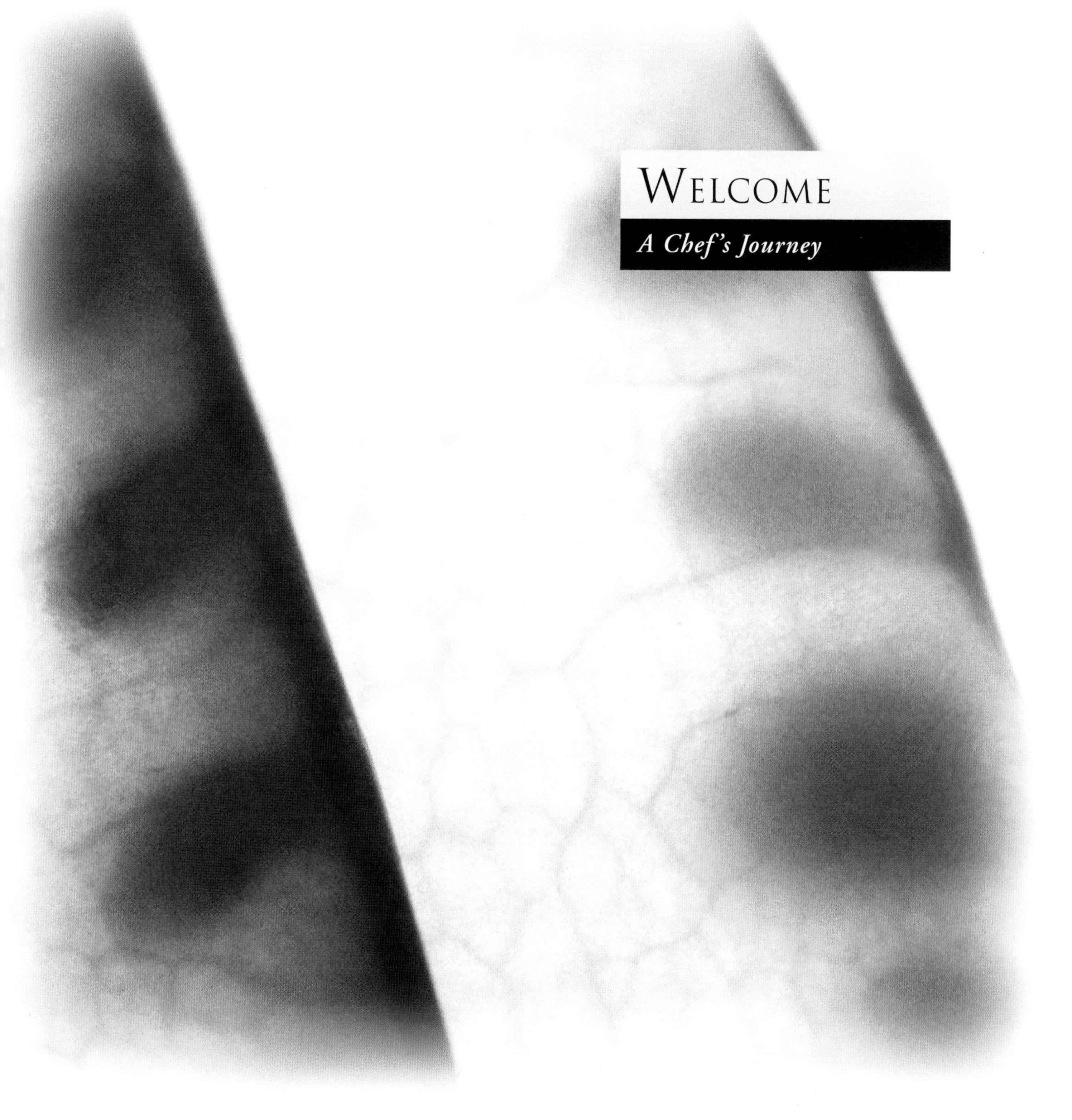

5:25 pm: Excitement is in the air. The kitchen is a beehive of last-minute activity as busy cooks scurry around preparing the many things that will be needed during the dinner rush. Aromas from pots on the stove mingle with the scent of freshly baked bread. The chef, a tall figure in white, is tasting new menu items and describing to the wait staff the nuances of a carrot sauce. One cook, having just returned from the garden, is washing salad greens, while another flashes a sharp knife as she minces sage leaves. An air of professionalism is evident, and everyone is intent on the work at hand. Moments later the pace picks up as the maitre d' enters and announces that the first guests of the evening have arrived.

Cuisine is art. Whether you are a patron of a renowned restaurant or enjoying the blue plate special at the corner diner, a chef directing a kitchen brigade or a tentative apprentice cook learning the fine points of slicing onions, a spirited home entertainer orchestrating yet another dinner party or a parent cooking supper for the kids — you can be a connoisseur of that art.

Cuisine, like art, demands passion and focus. Cuisine highlights craft and celebrates creativity. It rewards discipline and integrity. It ranges from subtle to bold and can offer a respite from the ordinary, an interlude from the mundane. At its best, cuisine elevates the beholder and the diner,

The chef at his station in the open kitchen.

enhancing the moment and inspiring appreciation.

Cuisine, too, is subject to the same pitfalls as art. Cuisine can suffer from overanalysis and pretension. It can be ill conceived, contrived, and lacking in character. Often cuisine is overhyped and full of contradiction, and can become static and predictable or even irrelevant. Worse yet, it may disappoint.

By embracing the responsibilities inherent in cuisine, the cook becomes an artist. Achieving this level is a simple matter. One need only commit to honest expression and the possibilities become endless. Expression is one of the core aspects of genuine hospitality: do what comes naturally, be yourself.

Ultimately, the best art and the most memorable cuisine are the simplest. While the simplicity of a preparation is not always apparent at first glance, it is always evident in the taste. Indeed, to appreciate the inherent ease with which some ingredients combine or the affinity a particular item may have for a specific technique takes a level of maturity that often eludes inexperienced cooks. Too often cooks focus on the presentation, the grand finale. Instead, if you focus on the base elements of an art form, master-pieces will result.

This book is about simplicity. It is a story of great ingredients and the methods they inspire. (There is more about equipment, ingredients, and methods in The Chef's Kitchen chapter.) It is a distillation of just one day in the life of a kitchen, a day that echoes the rhythms of the surrounding countryside. It is a study of how easily cuisine becomes art.

8:30 pm: The kitchen is alive! "Table 3 is fired, table 9 is on the rail, pick up 7, going to the plate on 14, fire veg for 6, how's that lamb shank?" shouts the chef, who seems to be doing 10 things at once. One glance at the action reveals a meticulously choreographed dance: five cooks are moving with an economy of motion bordering on ballet, flames are leaping from the grill, somewhere a funky jazz beat is booming from a speaker, the wait staff are whisking plates in and out of the kitchen, and the dishwashers are furiously trying to stay ahead of the rising tide. An anxious cook presents two plates for the chef's inspection before they are taken to the guests. The chef pauses, wipes an imaginary smudge from the rim, and, grinning, announces, "Perfect!" The cook returns to his station beaming. Everyone is having a terrific time!

As a child growing up in New York, I didn't realize that the culinary habits of my family were preparing me for a lifetime of cuisine. My life was an unending series of special occasions, all with unique foods. We lived in the midst of apple country in New York's Hudson Valley, and every fall my mom would bake heavenly apple pies. To this day I judge all pies against hers! She would spend hours every Sunday preparing feasts that were served with all the pomp and circumstance of a fine restaurant. My brothers and I were

As in most kitchens, there's just enough room to get the job done.

my world, only homemade goodness that was irresistible.

In all of this kitchen activity I was a willing participant and often helped with the cooking. I enjoyed it very much and even had a small collection of cookbooks. On one occasion, I became captivated with the notion of a seven-course meal and researched its particulars. With the aid of my brothers I prepared and served a truly memorable meal composed of unpronounceable French wines and dishes. I wrote an elegant menu by hand for each of the eight guests. This marked my world debut as a chef. I had no culinary aspirations — cooking was just something fun to do.

even allowed a glass of wine to enjoy with our dinner. My dad always made sure that the plates were hot, a concept that was lost on me at the time, but one that consumes me now. He was also responsible for taking us to innumerable restaurants that were always thrilling. I'll never forget the first time I ordered filet mignon; I felt so sophisticated!

My mom's influence on my perception of food and its inherent goodness has been profound. From birthday dinners, hot cross buns at Easter, turkey with the trimmings at Thanksgiving, fish chowder and roast beef at Christmas, homemade snacks at Little League games, and alfalfa sprouts in my lunchbox sandwiches I learned that cooking is sharing. There was no fast food or cake mixes in

For years, I had been doing drawings of nature. Eventually, my artistic and creative tendencies led me to art school, and off I went to become a graphic designer. Deadlines and assignments didn't inspire me, however, and, when a new car necessitated income, I took the first job available: cooking in a local restaurant. I didn't realize it was the first step of a journey that would include illustrating my own cookbook years later. The rest, as they say, is history.

Through a series of lucky breaks and steadily diminishing interest in art school, I found myself a cook in what represented the pinnacle of fine dining in my college town: a very good hotel dining room. I stayed for a year and a half and learned everything I could from a chef whom I worshipped. I loved my job and was good at it. I read voraciously, progressed steadily, and before long was working the prestigious sauté station and having the time of my life. I was even allowed to create special dishes and developed my affinity for inventing new preparations. Based on my ambition and the reputation of the restaurant, I was offered a head chef's position at another local restaurant. I leaped at the chance to be my own boss.

I was 20 years old and responsible for a 165-seat dining room. It was a disaster. No one had taught me the fundamentals of being a manager, and, when my cooks expected me to know all the answers, I began questioning the basis of my cuisine. I trusted my cooking experience but not my knowledge. It was time to get serious. Six months later I enrolled at the Culinary Institute of America.

At the CIA I discovered a previously hidden world of commonsense cooking and fundamentals. Before, I had learned specific cooking methods to satisfy the chef. Now, I was learning how to cook to satisfy the ingredients. There was nothing arbitrary about what I learned — it was all insightful and ingredient driven. I learned culinary history and worked with myriad different chefs and ingredients, all with something unique to teach me. One of my classes covered the vast

The chef details every plate that his kitchen produces.

subject of wine and its place at the table. After class I spent all my time in passionate debate with my fellow students, extolling the virtues of one method over another. The CIA was a culinary Mecca and tremendously exciting.

While at the school I had the opportunity to work with two notable chefs. As an extern I landed a plum position at Larry Forgione's restaurant An American Place in Manhattan. I was cooking in the big leagues, which was a dream come true! Larry was one of the most prominent cooks in America and well known for his passionate devotion to regional cuisine. He had a profound influence on my developing style and inspired me to continue evolving as a cook. When I graduated, I was invited to serve a fellowship at the school's flagship restaurant The American Bounty. There I worked with Paul Sartory, who had the most profound influence on me of all the chefs I have worked with. Paul taught me how to think about cuisine and its creation. He solidified all of my convictions regarding food and the atmosphere in which it should be enjoyed. He also taught me an all-encompassing responsibility to respect my ingredients.

I left the school with a tremendous sense of confidence and ability, knowing that I was embarking on a lifetime's worth of learning and culinary adventures. My first stop was

London, where I encountered that peculiar species of chef — autocratic and uninspiring — that inhabits the classical Michelin starred restaurants of Europe. I spent a brief period despising my role as a cog in the vast culinary machine of Le Gavroche, pouring cream into everything I cooked and wondering how the restaurant was so highly regarded when its food was so boring. I escaped my shackled existence and touched down at David Bouley's eponymous temple in Manhattan. Happily enjoying my position working in one of the most elite restaurants on the globe, I heard about a sleepy country inn in Canada that needed a chef for the summer. Once again it was time to move on.

11:00 pm: The controlled chaos has subsided, and the last desserts of the evening are being served. A relaxed atmosphere, punctuated by backslapping and horseplay, has settled over the brigade. Some of the cooks are cleaning up the kitchen, a monumental task considering the volume of food prepared this evening. Ninety-two guests dined tonight, some of them enjoying the seven-course Chef's Tasting Menus; well over three hundred plates of meticulously crafted cuisine were served. The chef is proudly showing off the kitchen and chatting with a group of enthusiastic guests who are mystified by the small space in which their meals were prepared. The sous-chef is reviewing tomorrow's menu and preparing a prep list, while another cook fills an enormous stock pot with roasted lamb bones that will simmer overnight and serve as a sauce base tomorrow. Everyone is tired but ebullient. Something magical happened here tonight, and tomorrow everyone will be part of the magic again.

The Inn at Bay Fortune is the preeminent country inn on Prince Edward Island. It rests on a hilltop overlooking the Fortune harbor and Northumber-land Strait beyond, evoking the maritime spirit for which the area is known. The Inn, which is open from May to October, showers its guests with traditional hospitality. Its

17 guest rooms are graciously inviting, and its restaurant has become world famous for contemporary creative cuisine in a country inn setting. While breakfast is served only to guests staying at the Inn, at dinnertime the restaurant is open to others. Lunch is not served.

In 1910 the Inn was built by Broadway playwright Elmer Harris as a retreat from the summer heat of New York. In later years, the actress Colleen Dewhurst graced its rooms. Innkeeper David Wilmer purchased the house in 1989 and restored it to its original splendor, reincarnated as a country inn.

When I joined the Inn in 1992 for its fourth season, it was my chance to create a utopian kitchen aesthetic with an intensely regional focus, something that previously I had only imagined. Prince Edward Island is a chef's paradise, an unspoiled beauty that provides countless culinary treasures. Within minutes of my kitchen are wild mushrooms and herbs, pristine waters teeming with fish, pastures of dairy herds and flocks of sheep, cheesemakers, flour millers, beekeepers, and vegetable farmers. I knew I had found something very special.

With the blessing of David Wilmer and the mandate to take the restaurant to the top, I set out to learn as much as I could about the great variety of food producers on the island. With my natural respect for ingredients, I saw the opportunity to learn the stories behind every item on my menu. I knew that there was tremendous potential for a dedicated chef, but even so, I underestimated just how great that opportunity was. By the end of my first year, I had fallen in love with the island and its abundance. There always seemed to be yet another producer to meet, and

An apprentice, Lance, shows off some muses, artfully presented morsels the guests are served before they are given menus.

each one had a unique product.

From the start we professed a "build it and they will come" attitude. Even though we were miles off the beaten track, we chose to create a fine dining establishment that encompassed all of the cutting-edge attitudes I had developed about food. We were not hesitant to cook provocative food and applied all the contemporary theories that were entrenched in big city restaurants but were alien to the countryside. A garden was planted to provide the herbs that were unavailable elsewhere. We built a wine cellar and began stocking it with wines new to the island. Each day was a blur as Team Cuisine, my kitchen staff, was formed and we focused on the details of the evening dinner service. The menu became a virtual tour of the island and reflected the vast bounty available to an intrepid chef; it also became a showcase for healthy cooking. We introduced the Chef's Tasting Menus, artistic presentation, cooking classes, wine tastings, and kitchen tours. Before long we were getting noticed!

As the years have passed, we have become a culinary destination. Our utopian ideals have continued to grow and the restaurant has matured dramatically. My cooking and core culinary beliefs have evolved, and the list of our suppliers has continued to lengthen. A thousand food stories have been told, promising many more. Our garden has grown and, with the work of a full-time staff, now provides all of our specialty vegetables and herbs. Our chef's table in the kitchen is the hottest ticket in town. To my delight, we have reached a level that attracts other passionate cooks, and Team Cuisine is an unmatched powerhouse of dedicated talent. Our hospitality is renowned, and we are under constant media scrutiny.

As we forge ahead, it is with a sense that hard work and devotion to ideals is rewarding. We recognize our fortune and are grateful for the opportunity we have to showcase our hospitality. Welcome to dining at The Inn at Bay Fortune!

Wines share top billing with the Inn's cuisine.

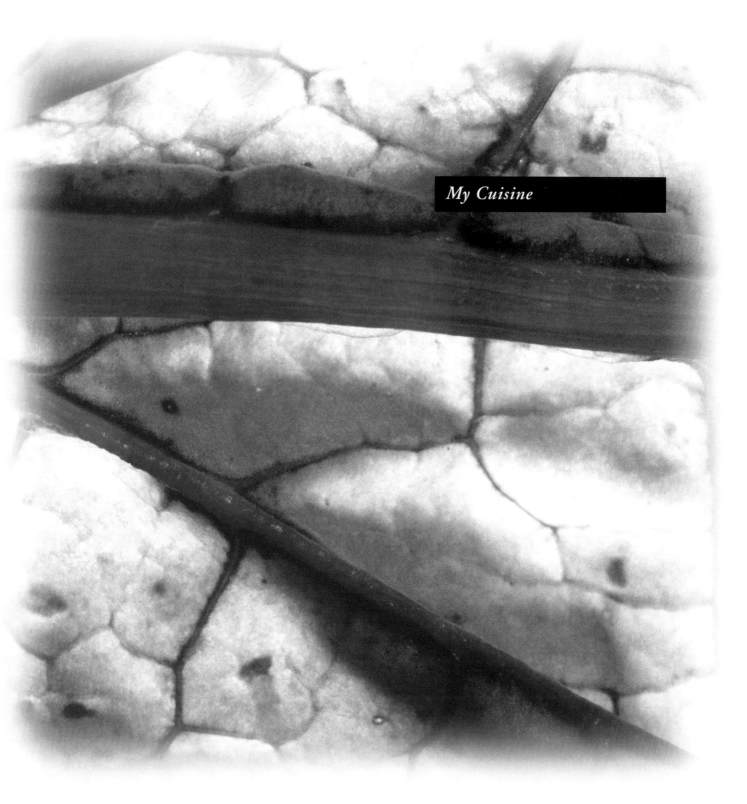

My Cuisine

8:30 am: The sun is just beginning to warm the ground as the chef, seeking inspiration, begins his morning stroll through the kitchen garden. He walks through the herb garden with Clarice, the gardener, and takes notes as they discuss the progress of some of the new herb varieties. Pausing, they crush the leaves of an exotic sage between their fingers and savor the resulting fragrance. There are about one hundred varieties of herbs to consider in the creation of the daily menu, and Clarice knows the exact status of each. Moving on toward the vegetable garden, they walk through a grove of apple trees that are being coaxed back from the wild. In the salad garden, neat, colorful rows of exotic looking salad greens are flourishing. Later in the day, the salad cook will trim a section of each. The chef listens as Clarice updates him on the progress of the wide variety of vegetables that the guests will enjoy that evening.

Cooking is a metaphor for life. Cooking rewards both the casual participant and the passionate creator. It is easy to begin but takes a lifetime to master. It celebrates simplicity and accommodates complexity. It inspires passion while allowing indifference. It can elevate the ordinary and make accessible the extraordinary.

Cooking is the only art form that challenges all five senses. The visual appeal of colorful ingredients and a chef's artistic presentation are as pleasing to the eye as nature itself. The crackle of sizzling bacon rewards the attentive ear. The mouthfeel of a smooth ripe persimmon is as sensuous as a lover's caress. The aroma of freshly baked bread or a chance hint of spice has the power to transport the beholder. Tasting a well-prepared dish can suggest cultures afar, invoke a smile, and inspire understanding.

It is not necessary to understand to appreciate. It is entirely possible to live a life of culinary adventure and blissfully ignore the elements of creation that accompany it. But for those cooks who truly embrace the art of cooking, no detail is too small, no ingredient too obscure, no method too difficult to satisfy their hunger for understanding.

I don't pretend to know all the answers. I can only share my mission in the hope that it will inspire you to embrace cooking as fervently as I do. Since my culinary journey has no end in sight, I am only able to describe where I am today.

I have distilled the essence of my cooking into three simple concepts: use great ingredients, treat them with respect, and share the result. I haven't always understood these precepts, and even now I continue to refine my application of them. But my career to date makes me confident that I'm on the right track.

Only great ingredients, treated with respect, are used.

When I first began cooking, I was too arrogant to use recipes. I viewed my creations as personal expression and was loath to dilute them with the expertise of others. My naiveté and misplaced confidence often caused hilarious results. I had never heard of cold soup, so gazpacho was heated before being served. Rapidly I learned that I had better toe the line and follow the recipe if I was going to stay employed! But I never lost my raw creativity; recipes were just something to be added to. My unwillingness to accept the status quo was a good quality, although I didn't realize it then.

For years my attitude was "more is better." In my hunt for the elusive goal of flavor perfection, I would add ingredient after ingredient to the simplest preparations. My signature tomato sauce had no less than 23 ingredients! My technique was steadily improving and I was not afraid to tackle any obscure method, but everything I made was complicated. I was convinced that the fine dining patrons I was serving were appreciative of the beautiful hodge-podge of ingredients on their plates. Unknowingly I was practicing a method-driven cuisine, and my first experiences as a chef only served to accelerate my quest for a unified theory to validate it.

The Culinary Institute of America served to awaken my latent passion. I was immersed in an atmosphere of absolute focus on all things culinary. Suddenly, theories that had been inexpressible were given voice. I began to replace the arbitrary nature of my craft with solid conviction and understanding.

For the first time I learned to celebrate my ingredients. I worked with chefs who were passionate about things as simple as an onion, not just any onion, but an organically grown onion of an heirloom variety. Almost overnight I was transformed! I realized that my ingredients were not coming from trucks and boxes but from the earth and sea, from the labors of others. I began to delve deeper and realized that it was the ingredients that were inspiring me, that they were my link to the full circle of cuisine. I also gained an appreciation for the important role that wine plays in fully realizing the subtle elements of cuisine. My cooking, which had previously been selfish and one-dimensional, became cooperative and mature. I felt a new responsibility to the ingredients, a responsibility to showcase them, to highlight them. I was laying the groundwork for what is now my ingredient-driven cuisine.

On many occasions, guests of the Inn have remarked that a particular dish was the best thing they had ever tasted and that they wonder what magic we were up to in the kitchen. Without exception what they are unknowingly reacting to is the quality of the ingredients we cook with. People may have become so used to lifeless tomatoes that our vine-ripened, warm-from-the-sun fresh fruit is an epiphany for them. Cooks are responsible only for 10 percent of a dish's character — the other 90 percent

The Inn's cuisine is driven by the ingredients.

is mother nature's domain. Our role is just to guide the ingredients through our kitchen and not impede their destiny. Cook with great ingredients, and your cuisine will shine!

I now define my creations by the ingredients they contain. My appreciation of the ingredients has grown into respect and has influenced me in many ways. Execution is now simple, whereas once I combined ingredients indiscriminately. My desire to highlight the essence of an ingredient inspires me to unite minimal complementary flavors. I am mesmerized by the diversity of varieties in the basil family and by other similar food phenomena. I analyze a recipe and remove ingredients to improve it. Presentations signal the respect for the raw product. No ingredient is too mundane to play a starring role; a carrot is an object to be revered.

My respect for ingredients has profoundly affected the methods and techniques of my cooking. My insistence on drawing natural flavors out of an ingredient has guided the procedures used in the kitchen. What was previously arbitrary is now insightful. Whole libraries of books now make sense. Why has replaced how. By learning the nuances of an ingredient and focusing intently on its characteristics my style has developed. The natural form of a vegetable is something to be celebrated, not automatically sliced, diced, chopped, puréed, and strained away. Respect your ingredients: they are what make your efforts a success.

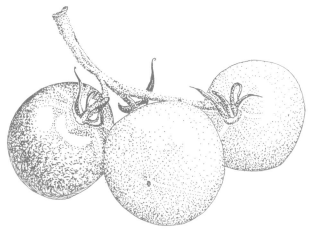

"Listen to your tomatoes for they have much to tell you; speak their language and they will share their secrets . . ."

The conveniences of modern society and the reality of urban life have distanced many cooks from the rhythms of nature. Often cooks approach their task from the wrong direction. Instead of using foods from nearby, they use ingredients from half a world away that have no relevance to the local geography or season. Have you ever eaten strawberry shortcake in January? Unless you were in a place where strawberries grow at that time, it was an unnatural thing to do. Cuisine is a celebration of here and now. There is nothing more satisfying than a trip to the market to search for inspiration.

We have become kitchen lemmings. Too often we blindly accept the assurances of a label. The sign says tomatoes, and therefore the hard, round, red object that resembles a billiard ball must be a tomato. Our shopping lists have become homogenized. Apples are available in two varieties: red and green. The average diet includes fewer than 40 items repeated day after day. All of these factors conspire to relegate ingredients to a secondary role in cuisine. A cook who achieves bland results after closely following a recipe does not question the authenticity of the ingredients, but instead assumes that a lack of skill in preparing the recipe is responsible.

It serves no purpose to adopt a high and mighty stance toward cuisine. Cooking is about sharing. My kitchen is dedicated to demystifying fine dining, removing it from its pedestal and making it accessible to all. We don't try to befuddle our guests with intimidating foreign words on our menu. Our wait staff can explain any preparation using ordinary words. We welcome comments from our guests and often invite them to come and see the kitchen action. We've even built a special glassed-in, air-conditioned room

In the kitchen, guests are a constant presence: the chef describes the menu.

within the kitchen for our chef's table, where eight people can dine in the kitchen. Our Chef's Tasting Menus entertain as well as enlighten. All of these factors are part of sharing our cuisine.

Cooking in a restaurant is fundamentally different from home cooking. In a restaurant such as ours, professionalism and responsibility are invigorating and inspire excellence. Perhaps the most distinguishing characteristic of my kitchen is the constant pressure to improve, to exceed expectations. The pace is furious but exhilarating. There is always an element of surprise in the air. Our spontaneity infuses our cuisine with a life of its own.

To be a great cook requires natural hospitality. The best home cooks and the best restaurant cooks have one important characteristic in common: both share their craft and strive to do the same thing — please their guests and themselves in the process.

4:15 pm: The chef is on the phone discussing the next day's dairy order with a local farmer. Jeff, the sous-chef, asks for the keys to the Jeep so that he can go and get some watercress needed for the cold side (the section of the kitchen that produces all the menu items that don't require heating or cooking). "I'll go with you," says the chef as he hangs up the phone. Just before he leaves he puts a pan of glazed walnuts in the oven.

They drive through the fields behind the Inn, pull up at a stream where a bed of wild watercress grows, and begin to harvest some of the succulent leaves. The scent of mint fills the air — in the midst of the watercress grow spearmint plants. Some have already been transplanted to the kitchen garden. Chef and sous-chef fill a container with pungent wild mint and head back to the kitchen. Arriving, the chef tastes the walnuts — perfect! Ten minutes have passed and the mise-en-place *(the many items that must be prepared before each mealtime) is several steps closer to being ready.*

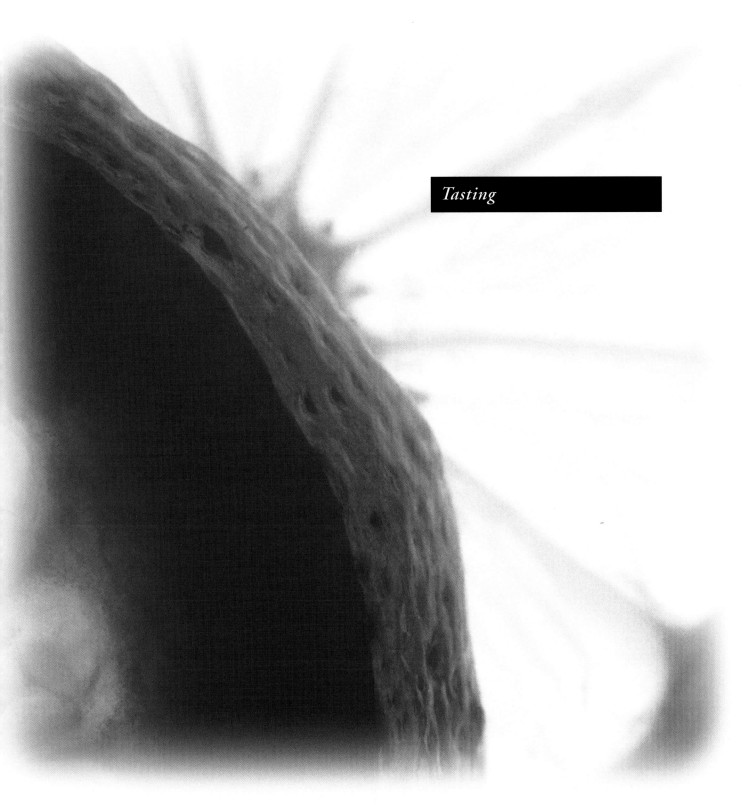

Tasting

12:05 pm: As the sun streams through the kitchen's open windows a breeze fills the air. One glance reveals a meticulously organized space that seems filled to capacity with every gadget imaginable. Gleaming counters are covered with cutting boards and knives. Shelves line one wall and are completely filled with the dry ingredients that serve as menu building blocks. Bottles of various vinegars and oils are beside a shelf filled with several kinds of honey. Garden fresh herbs and vegetables, their scents mingling in the air, rest in baskets. Another shelf is dedicated to chocolate — dark, milk, white, and other exotic varieties. On a long ledge that spans the entire wall are neatly labeled jars containing the spices of the world. A cook is lost in thought, pondering his choices as he scans the spices looking for inspiration.

The ability to taste is the most important skill that any cook possesses. Tasting is our link between ingredients and technique, our portal to culinary perception. Tasting provides us with a view of the world's culinary possibilities, one ingredient at a time. The nuances of wine and the subtleties of cheese would be lost without tasting. Culinary triumph would be indistinguishable from culinary fiasco.

Although tasting is integral to being a good cook, it rarely gets the attention it merits. Many professional cooks are more focused on their knife handling skills or the speed with which they can produce a meal than on how well they are able to discern the flavor of their preparations. In fact, it is common practice to prepare a dish and not taste it at all. Have you ever dined out and thought that you could do a better job if you were in the kitchen?

Humans developed the ability to taste long before there were restaurants and chefs. When we were still hunters and gatherers, it was important to be able to discern the characteristics of foods. It was survival, not enjoyment, that motivated us. We had to distinguish between harmful and helpful foodstuffs, and we developed the ability to remember a certain flavor and the effect of specific foods on our health. All of our tasting abilities can be traced to our evolution.

As civilization has progressed, we have maintained our instinctive abilities. But now dining for pleasure often replaces eating for sustenance. We celebrate the planet's vast array of ingredients, anywhere, anytime. We are exposed to far more tastes than our ancestors ever encountered, but we still taste in much the same way that they did.

While most cooks are familiar with tasting, few understand it. Tasting is the process of perceiving the flavor and other characteristics of an ingredient or preparation. Flavor represents the overall combination of tastes, aromas, mouthfeel, and temperature of an ingredient or preparation. These are easy concepts to understand, but it can take a lifetime to appreciate their subtleties.

The key to tasting is doing it! I am often asked by guests of the Inn or by other cooks what my secret is, what magical ability I have. My answer is that it's just tasting experience. For years I have taken every opportunity to taste new things or to retaste the familiar. Over time I couldn't help but build up a resource that is part of my cooking style. I urge you to do the same: taste everything you can and learn from your experiences. Be analytical, look for and understand nuances in flavor. Overcome your natural aversion to the unknown, and embrace the novelty of a new experience.

There are myriad factors to consider when tasting. By understanding and applying all of them, you will be well on

The chef in his "studio" — the kitchen.

your way to cooking like a pro. But above all, don't allow your analysis of food — yours or someone else's — to diminish your simple enjoyment of it.

TASTE

A series of highly specific physio-chemical reactions occur when we perceive flavor. The primary reaction point for this process is the taste bud, which interacts at the molecular level with the food we eat. Our mouths are full of taste buds, our cheeks, the roof of our mouth, and even the backs of our throat all have them. The tongue has the highest density and is the primary tasting tool chiefly because it's mobile. There are five primary taste sensations.

SWEET

Sweetness indicates the presence of energy-giving calories. Without caloric intake we would die; scientists theorize that this need is responsible for our hard-wired enjoyment of sweets. The front of our tongue is most sensitive to sweetness. When our ancestors tentatively touched their tongue to something unfamiliar, they could taste it without actually ingesting anything. Chances were that if it was sweet, it was worth eating.

> ### TASTE TEST
> ✳
> Try this experiment: Dip your finger into your favorite sauce and taste it, then use a spoon to taste the same sauce. Which method was more telling? My cooks are trained to use a spoon, as doing so gives them a better opportunity to be analytical.

SOUR

Acidic foods such as citrus fruits and vinegars taste sour. In low concentrations, sourness is pleasing to most people, especially when it is balanced with sweetness. The low pH value that corresponds with sourness can signify decomposition of foods in the wild. This is valuable knowledge to a foraging diner.

SALT

We are very sensitive to sodium chloride, a necessary component of our diet, and can detect it in extremely low concentrations. It serves as a flavor enhancer and, when used properly, balances various flavors.

BITTER

Bitterness signifies the presence of potentially harmful alkaloids, which have high pH values. The back of our tongues is sensitive to bitterness. Something that is very bitter, perhaps even toxic, will induce an instinctive gag reflex, which is a natural defense mechanism against poisoning. We have learned to tolerate and even enjoy slight bitterness in many foods, such as chocolate and coffee. The extreme bitterness of some poisonous things in nature warns us that they are inedible.

UMAMI

Umami, a Japanese word for which there is no English equivalent, is the rich, meaty taste that characterizes a perfectly cooked steak. The least understood of the taste sensations, *umami* is linked to the amino acids used by plants and animals to build proteins, another necessary

> ### TASTE TEST
> ✳
> Try this experiment: taste granulated sugar, sea salt, white vinegar, and tonic water. The four pure taste sensations will be evident.

part of our diet. *Umami* is also found in other foods such as shiitake mushrooms, and in monosodium glutamate (MSG). Western culture does not generally recognize the notion of *umami,* but it is becoming more prevalent in contemporary culinary thinking. As scientists and chefs continue to apply their resources to understanding it, *umami* will become more known globally.

There are also two secondary taste sensations.

HEAT

Stimulation created in our mouths by spicy foods is perceived as heat. The compound capsaicin, present in peppers, is responsible for this effect. When used properly as a flavor enhancer, pepper is an integral part of cooking.

COLD

The cooling effect that menthol has on our mouth is very pleasant. Menthol is a natural compound present in mint and actually deadens our taste buds by numbing them. In many of the world's cuisines, mint is often found in conjunction with spicy foods.

AROMA

Although taste sensations are important to the perception of flavor, aromas provide the character, the nuances, the undertones that define it. To cook well, it is critical to understand and appreciate the role that aromas play. Many of the recipes in this book include methods that are designed to maximize the aromatic properties of foods.

MOUTHFEEL

The way a food feels in your mouth can heighten your enjoyment of it. A meal would be boring if it was composed entirely of purées, regardless of how flavorful they were. We enjoy the texture of meat, the smoothness of chocolate, the crackle of a roast chicken's skin, or the crunch of a potato chip. Mouthfeel can also be an indication of ripeness; some fruits, such as persimmon and avocado, develop an amazing smoothness. An apple progresses from hard and crisp to mealy and soft as it matures. Skilled chefs provide contrast in their creations. At the Inn, I try to have a crisp element as part of almost every menu item to contrast with the smooth sauces and other textures of the dishes.

TEMPERATURE

The temperature at which an ingredient is served has a profound effect on our perception of flavor. One of the most common complaints about a restaurant's food is that it's not hot or cold enough. A cook's creation can be perfectly executed but won't be appreciated if it's served at the wrong temperature. The temperature of a food can be comforting: steaming hot chocolate in the winter or cold iced tea in the summer are culinary classics.

Food that is very cold numbs your taste buds, making it hard to taste. You can compensate for this by overseason-

Elegant simplicity: Chardonnay ice and a delicate pansy.

ing a preparation that will be served very cold or frozen. Anything that is too hot will burn your mouth and can actually kill taste buds (fortunately, they regenerate rapidly). The flavors in food are most perceptible when it is at body temperature. One of the reasons chocolate is so universally appealing is that its melting point is almost the same as your body temperature. Preparations with contrasting temperatures can be very pleasing — few things rival a hot fudge sundae!

FLAVOR ENHANCERS

There are some ingredients that will enhance the flavor of a dish without contributing any flavor of their own. These ingredients are known as flavor enhancers. The most common are salt and pepper.

TASTE TEST
✳

Try this experiment: Pinch your nose and bite into an apple. Chew for a few moments and note the relative sweetness and sourness. Also note the apple's blandness: its taste has no character. Now release your nostrils and enjoy the apple's flavor.

When used sparingly, salt is undetectable, but its effect is dramatic. It has the unique ability to make the natural flavors present in the ingredients of a preparation more vibrant and defined, and can mold a group of seemingly disparate tastes into a cohesive flavor. Salt is especially useful in helping define less flavorful ingredients such as potatoes, rice, or even the flours in bread. All types of cooking, including pastry making and baking, benefit from the judicious use of salt.

Salt is an indispensable part of cooking and should not be dismissed because of its reputed ill effects on health. Even when used in moderation, salt can impart its unique properties to any dish. At the Inn, everything we cook is seasoned with an appropriate amount of salt. There are no

Superb cuisine demands focus and precision.

salt shakers on the tables; it is the kitchen's job to season the food. I often watch with amazement as diners in other restaurants reach for the salt before tasting their food. They give salt a bad name!

Pepper is one of the most fascinating ingredients used in cuisine, and like salt, its unique properties are easily understood and applied. There are many different types of peppers, but they all share the same characteristics when used properly. While the burning, spicy, hot sensations created by pepper can be enjoyable, its use in smaller concentrations is universally appealing. Pepper stimulates your palate. Just as your eyes react to sudden movement and your ears to sudden noises, pepper "wakes up" your taste buds. When all your taste buds are on alert and sending signals to the brain, you sense more flavors. There is not more flavor to taste; you are simply tasting more of what flavor there is. Pepper makes everything taste livelier.

If you can tolerate the burning sensation of chili peppers and hot sauces made from them, a world of intriguing flavors will be open to you. Peppers vary in heat, and range from mild poblanos through medium to explosive habaneros. Your reward for the burn is the accompanying flavor. You will also enjoy the endorphins, pleasure chemicals that your brain produces to counteract the pain — they produce a mild euphoria!

Due to their pungency, other ingredients can have the effect of pepper. Horseradish, when used undiluted, is very potent. Ginger adds a mystical note. Many other spices in high concentrations can also be piquant. Pure cinnamon oil, the characteristic ingredient in "red hot" candy, adds heat to one of our ice creams.

ACHIEVING FLAVOR BALANCE

If flavor results from the combination of tastes, aromas, and other factors, how do we control it? How does a cook determine that a dish is finished, that its overall flavor is polished? Assuming that great ingredients have been used and that they have been treated properly, the last adjustments to a preparation can dramatically alter its flavor.

The basic flavor of a dish is established with the choice of high quality ingredients and the well conceived method used to prepare them. The seasoning stage of a preparation, which does not necessarily occur last, is the time to fine tune or enhance that flavor. The finished dish offers much opportunity for analysis: a thoughtful taste of the preparation just before serving may inspire an adjustment, either at that moment or the next time the dish is made.

Cuisine benefits from balance. A group of preparations that are served together must both complement and contrast with each other. The palate is dulled when assailed by a progression of like tastes; variety is pleasing. The first thought that crosses my mind as I taste is whether I sense balance. If what I am tasting is to be served alone, then the balance should be in my mouth; if it is to be served with other elements, then they too must be tasted to assess the net

effect. I actually scroll through the taste sensations in my mind, analyzing each in turn. The following are some of the factors I consider:

* Is the dish seasoned properly? Could it benefit from a bit more salt or pepper? Are the flavors clear and defined?
* Is the dish characterized predominantly by only one of the taste sensations? Is it too salty, sweet, bitter, or sour? If so, are there other balancing elements on the plate? If not, what can be added to achieve balance?
* Does the dish taste the way it should? Does it meet the expectations of its name? Are the major ingredients obvious or subtle?
* Is one ingredient too dominant, hiding the others?
* Do the herbs or spices complement the whole?
* Is the dish the proper temperature?
* Is the dish too rich or too bland?

Adding just a bit more of a particular taste element — a splash of vinegar, a spoonful of honey, a pinch of salt, or a few grinds of pepper — often can balance a preparation. If the flavor is too subtle, adjusting the seasoning can improve the clarity.

Not only the primary taste sensations must be balanced. Flavors, too, must be in accord. One of the most appealing and intriguing aspects of creating cuisine is finding and pairing seemingly disparate ingredients. A unique flavor combination can define a dish, elevating it from food to cuisine. Every creative chef is searching for the next great dish

---

TASTE TEST
✳

Try this experiment: In succession taste iodized table salt, kosher salt, and pure sea salt. Which do you prefer? The additives in table salt give it a powerful chemical flavor that can be very unappealing. At the Inn, we only use pure sea salt, ground daily.

---

to rival tomatoes with basil. With discipline, innovative harmony is possible. This discipline results from experienced tasting, from discerning complementary nuances that are not immediately apparent.

Over the years I have tried many different taste combinations, and I hope I have progressed from creativity for its own sake to genuine insight. Although every possible culinary avenue probably has been explored already by others, my own independent quest continues to define my cuisine. My approach to cooking demands careful attention to taste. If two ingredients are used together, they must be individually apparent while simultaneously transformed. The genesis of a dish can begin with the simple desire to marry flavors.

Each of the following food combinations represents a starting point for exploration. They all appear in recipes in this book, but they can also be used in many other different ways. Each combination is distinctive and is the result of applied tasting. Some of them are obvious, others less so. From simple pairings such as these an entire dish can evolve.

* Rosemary and vanilla
* Peas and basil
* Horseradish and nutmeg
* Carrot and cinnamon
* Peach and sage
* Pear and coriander
* Lentils and single malt Scotch

TASTE TEST
✳
Try this experiment: Purée a ripe tomato in a blender. Taste it. Add, tasting after each addition, a pinch of salt, a few grinds of fresh pepper, a few drops of lemon juice, and a sprinkle of sugar. What did you observe? How did the tomato improve in flavor after each addition?

* Tomato and ginger
* Rhubarb and anise
* Chocolate and pepper

A recipe offers guidelines and is only a beginning. Words on paper cannot replace the active participation and thoughtfulness of the cook; the insight and reasons behind the methods are more important than blindly following instructions. There is always room for further interpretation and development. The results achieved in my kitchen will not be duplicated exactly in yours as you use this book. I urge you to personalize each recipe with touches of your own. Perhaps you don't share my affinity for a particular spice in a particular dish. Try something else! Let your own instincts be as compelling as the recipe.

Sous-chef Jeff McCourt aims for perfection.

1:15 pm: The chef is describing a new menu item to a cook. "Okay, for the pear chutney I want you to use a ratio of one onion for each pear, make a caramel, sweat the onions in it until they are glazed golden, season with nutmeg and vanilla, remember it's pear not vanilla nutmeg chutney, taste it, and balance it with red wine vinegar, salt, and Tabasco. Add the pears and just heat them through."

USING THE RECIPES

Recipes mean different things to professional and amateur cooks. Many chefs communicate recipes to their cooks in an abbreviated fashion, emphasizing control points and trusting their staff's culinary judgment. Many of the details given in written recipes are not necessary in a professional kitchen where the trained eye of a cook watches the progress of a preparation. In written recipes, however, timing becomes a question of minutes, and not one of how the preparation is actually evolving. Detailed instructions replace instinct. Often a desired result can be achieved in several ways, but a recipe can only reflect one of them. A recipe eliminates the flow of consciousness and spontaneity that is characteristic of many chefs when they are creating. The definitiveness of a recipe implies a need to follow it precisely or the results will fail. So why write recipes?

I want to share my cuisine, and my recipes are a form of that hospitality. My kitchen has many unique characteristics. I have allowed them to influence the way I have written this book. I want your cooking to reflect the spirit of our open kitchen. The menu items and recipes in this book were chosen to reflect the wide range of daily culinary tasks at The Inn at Bay Fortune. The recipes were gathered in my kitchen from the many that exist there, and have evolved from kitchen lingo and chef-speak to carefully crafted, ingredient-based methods. The following tips will aid your culinary journey.

* Read each menu item thoroughly before beginning preparation. Get a sense of the timing of the recipes that make up the menu item, and have your ingredients, your *mise-en-place,* ready.

* If you really want to duplicate the cuisine of the Inn, stock your kitchen with great ingredients. Spend a little more if need be. Remember, you have control of most of the flavor of a preparation as you gather its components. The results will reflect the ingredients used.

* Use your good culinary sense. Many variables in your environment, such as your equipment, tools, ingredients, and kitchen, will affect your efforts. Use these variables to your advantage.

* The recipes in this book reflect only one point in the ongoing development of cuisine at The Inn at Bay Fortune. Don't treat them as static. Use them, modify them, let them evolve in your kitchen.
* In the recipes, eggs are large, butter is unsalted, cream is heavy, meats and fish are perfect, fruit is ripe, vegetables are garden grown, herbs and spices are fresh, all salt is sea salt, and pepper is freshly ground. Every ingredient should represent an opportunity for excellence.
* Focus on your craft. Watch the ingredients as you follow the steps in preparing the recipes, and make adjustments if needed. Be patient and precise. Sweat the details.

Presentation: the final flourish.

* In some multipart menu items, a Timing section indicates the timing needed for preparing the various recipes included. Often several recipes may need to be underway simultaneously. If so, follow their instructions and the Timing hints carefully.
* Have fun with the presentation of the food you prepare. This type of cuisine inspires artful presentation. Follow the guidelines and add your own flair.
* Above all, enjoy yourself. Cooking is fun! Invite a friend to join you, put on some good music, pour a glass of wine, relax, and let your cuisine flow.

*"Experience is the surest guide in all culinary matters.
For no matter how detailed the theory may have been given,
it cannot do more than outline the basic principles,
it cannot replace the telling glance and the
know-how which come only from long practice."*

— Auguste Escoffier, 1907

MORNING

Bread and Breakfast

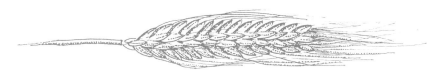

6:00 am: The kitchen is cold and silent. Dew lingers on the herb garden as the sun peeks over the eastern horizon. Bay Fortune is still a place where roosters crow as the day begins.

Breakfast offers the perfect opportunity to begin the day on a positive note. The slate is clean, the mind is clear, the body is rested. What better way to get started than with a tasty, wholesome meal made from familiar ingredients creatively prepared. Breakfast should not be provocative or challenging, but it can be fun. At the Inn we like to serve familiar dishes at breakfast, but we always include a twist and innovative presentation. Our guests love the attention to detail and always leave the dining room smiling, ready to enjoy their day.

The hands are a cook's most valuable tool.

7:00 am: The coffee is brewed, and the gardener is enjoying a cup before she heads out to pick the day's herbs. The ovens are on and gradually the kitchen is coming alive. The breakfast cook is mixing a huge bowl of pancake batter and discussing the merits of maple syrup with the gardener. The kitchen is becoming a gathering place. As the first guests of the day straggle in, they are greeted with the scent of rising bread mingling with that of sizzling bacon. The chef arrives and is soon eating granola as he begins to organize the day's activities.

We bake all of our bread during the morning. This is done both to maximize the use of our ovens and because the kitchen is relatively calm then. Rising bread can be disturbed by the chaos of the dinner cooks rushing about the kitchen in the afternoon. Our breads are meant to complement our guests' meals and to play a supporting role in the overall production. We tend not to bake with distracting herbs and other additions, and strive for earthy, neutral flavors. Occasionally a particular menu item will include a specific bread, such as our Black Pepper Yeast Bread (page 48).

10:25 am: Breakfast is over and the dishwasher is sweeping the floor for the third of many times during the day. Constant discipline keeps the kitchen shining. The members of Team Cuisine are whooping it up over their breakfast. The skirmishes and victories of the previous evening are being recounted and debated in great detail. One of the cooks is very proud of his perfect record for roasting meat and vows to maintain his record for the remainder of his assignment to the meat station. Another is mystified by the trouble she had with a tricky sabayon sauce and is asking for advice on the method. Everyone is excited and anxious to begin the day's tasks. The chef is working his way through a list of necessary phone calls before he drives off to pick up lamb from the sheep farm. He joins Team Cuisine to discuss the highlights of the coming day and the members' roles in the production.

Chive Biscuits with Scrambled Egg Stuffing, Cheddar Sauce, and Bacon

This dish combines a common group of breakfast ingredients in an interesting manner. Very few foods can rival the degree of hospitality evoked by freshly baked biscuits. These fluffy biscuits are simple to make and a great way to start the day.

6 SERVINGS

CHEF'S HINTS

It shouldn't take much longer than 30 seconds to process the dough. The most common mistake in biscuit making is overworking the dough; you should knead it only long enough to bring it completely together. ✳ To make cleanup a breeze and keep the dough from sticking to everything it touches, make sure your hands and work surfaces are lightly floured. ✳ Instead of using a rolling pin, you can use your hands to pat the dough to the right thickness. ✳ If you don't have a biscuit cutter, use a large soup can from which both ends have been removed.

CHIVE BISCUITS

3 cups all-purpose flour
2 tablespoons baking powder
1 teaspoon black pepper
1 teaspoon salt

½ pound butter, cubed and chilled (1 cup)
½ cup snipped chives
¾ cup milk
1 cup grated sharp cheddar cheese

PREHEAT the oven to 450°F. Grease a baking sheet.

SIFT together the flour, baking powder, pepper, and salt until thoroughly mixed. Place the flour mixture in the bowl of a food processor, add the butter, and process until completely combined.

PLACE the mixture in a bowl, add the chives, and stir to combine. Form a well in the center of the mixture and pour in the milk. Stir just until the mixture comes together into a sticky dough. It may be necessary to add 1 or 2 tablespoons of milk. The dough should come free from the sides of the bowl.

TURN the dough out onto a lightly floured surface. Sprinkle the dough with flour and knead gently just until it stays together. Roll the dough with a floured rolling pin to a thickness of 1 inch. Use a large biscuit cutter dipped in flour to cut out the biscuits. Reform the scraps and repeat until all the dough is used.

PLACE the biscuits 1 inch apart on the baking sheet and sprinkle cheese on top of each one. Bake until lightly browned, 12 to 15 minutes. Leave the oven on for cooking the bacon and the eggs. The biscuits may be wrapped in a towel and kept warm, or warmed in a hot oven just before being served.

CHEDDAR SAUCE

1 cup heavy cream
1 cup milk
3 tablespoons cornstarch
½ teaspoon ground nutmeg

½ teaspoon black pepper
½ teaspoon salt
2 cups grated sharp cheddar cheese

PLACE the cream, milk, cornstarch, nutmeg, pepper, and salt in a saucepan. Place the saucepan over medium heat and stir the mixture with a whisk. Continue stirring until the mixture thickens and begins to simmer. Add the cheese and stir until it is completely combined. Remove the sauce from the heat, cover it, and keep it warm until ready to serve.

BACON

12 slices thick-cut smoked bacon

ARRANGE the bacon slices in groups of 2 on a baking pan, folding each slice in half and allowing it to slightly overlap the adjacent slice.

BAKE for 10 to 12 minutes, turning the pan several times, until the bacon is crisp and done to your preference. Place the bacon on paper towels, and keep it warm until ready to serve.

CHEF'S HINTS

Use a very sharp, aged cheddar cheese for maximum flavor. A milder cheese will yield a bland sauce. ✳ If you are a big fan of nutmeg, try adding a little bit more.

SCRAMBLED EGG STUFFING

12 eggs	1 teaspoon salt
½ cup milk	Black pepper
⅔ cup snipped chives	3 tablespoons butter

WHISK the eggs and milk together completely. Whisk in ½ cup of the chives and the salt, and season with a little pepper.

MELT the butter in a large, ovenproof sauté pan over medium heat. Pour in the egg mixture. Quickly stir with a wooden spoon until the eggs begin to clump into small curds. Stir a moment longer, then place the pan in the still hot oven.

BAKE about 5 minutes until the eggs are just cooked. Remove the pan and cut the eggs into 6 wedges. Serve immediately.

PRESENTATION

(See the color photo illustrating the presentation of this dish.)

Chive oil (page 68)

PULL each biscuit apart into 2 equal pieces. Place the bottom piece on a warm plate. Place a scrambled egg wedge on the biscuit bottom. Ladle ¼ cup of the sauce over each scrambled egg wedge. Add several slices of crisp bacon and cap with the biscuit top. Garnish with the remaining chives and a dash of chive oil.

Country Inn Pancakes with Warm Blueberry Compote and Maple Whipped Cream

These are the gold standard of pancakes — light, golden, and fluffy with crisp edges.

4 SERVINGS

TIMING: Prepare the pancake batter and refrigerate at least 60 minutes, or overnight. ✳ Make the compote and the whipped cream. ✳ Cook the pancakes.

Warm Blueberry Compote

4 cups blueberries, fresh or frozen
1 cup sugar
2 tablespoons cornstarch

2 teaspoons vanilla
Juice and zest of 1 lemon

COMBINE the blueberries, sugar, cornstarch, vanilla, and lemon juice and zest in a saucepan. Place it over medium heat, and stir the blueberry mixture until thickened, allowing it to simmer briefly. Keep the compote in a warm place until you are ready to serve it.

Maple Whipped Cream

1½ cups heavy cream

6 tablespoons maple syrup

WHIP the cream and maple syrup together until the mixture forms stiff peaks. Refrigerate the maple whipped cream until you are ready to serve it.

CHEF'S HINTS

Citrus zesting tools can be bought at any good kitchenware store. Remove as much of the zest as possible from the fruit without digging into the white pith just beneath the skin — it is bitter. ✳ For an extra rich sauce, whisk in 4 tablespoons of butter just after removing the sauce from the heat.

COUNTRY INN PANCAKES

4 cups all-purpose flour	1 teaspoon ground nutmeg
2 tablespoons baking powder	4 eggs
2 tablespoons raw sugar*	½ pound butter, melted (1 cup)
1 tablespoon salt	2½ cups milk
1 teaspoon ground cinnamon	1 teaspoon vanilla

Raw sugar, which has a hint of molasses and is less processed than granulated sugar, is available in many supermarkets and specialty food stores.

SIFT together the flour, baking powder, sugar, salt, cinnamon, and nutmeg.

IN a separate bowl, beat the eggs thoroughly with a whisk. Add ½ cup of the butter and mix completely. Add the milk and vanilla and mix again.

FORM a well in the center of the dry ingredients. Pour in the egg mixture. Combine the mixtures with a few quick strokes, leaving the batter slightly lumpy. Cover the batter and refrigerate for a minimum of 60 minutes, or overnight if possible.

HEAT a large, nonstick skillet over medium heat until water drops dance on it. They should not disappear or sit and simmer. Pour 2 tablespoons of the remaining butter into the skillet, and, using the tip of a spoon, quickly pour in enough batter to form pancakes about 4 to 5 inches wide. When bubbles start to form on top of the pancakes, lift the edges and check for browning. When browned, turn the pancakes over quickly — don't hesitate! Finish cooking the pancakes and repeat the process with the remaining butter and batter. The finished pancakes may be covered with a towel and kept in a warm oven briefly while the others cook. Serve immediately when the last ones are cooked.

PRESENTATION

As soon as they are all cooked, arrange the pancakes on 4 warm plates. Ladle warm blueberry compote over the pancakes, place a large dollop of the maple whipped cream on top, and serve immediately.

Whole Wheat Apple Flipjacks with My Mom's Applesauce, Caramel Butter, and Bacon Roast Apples

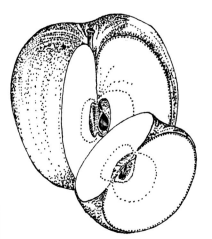

This is a special occasion breakfast. It's a little bit complicated, but the results are worth it. The flipjacks have a pleasing savory flavor enhanced by the lack of sugar in the batter.

6 SERVINGS

TIMING: Make the applesauce and let stand overnight. ✳ Prepare the roast apples and freeze for at least 2 hours, or overnight. ✳ Make the caramel butter. ✳ Make the flipjack batter. ✳ Bake the roast apples. ✳ Prepare the apples and baking pans for the flipjacks. ✳ Bake the flipjacks and warm the applesauce.

My Mom's Applesauce

½ cup sugar

¼ cup water

6 Granny Smith apples with skins, cored and chopped (about 9 to 10 cups)

½ cup cider

Juice and zest of 1 lemon

1 large cinnamon stick

½ teaspoon grated fresh ginger

½ teaspoon ground nutmeg

¼ teaspoon salt

FOLLOWING the instructions on page 67, form a caramel with the sugar and water, and then "shock" the hot caramel with the apples and cider. Let the mixture stand for a few minutes off the heat.

ADD the lemon juice and zest, cinnamon stick, ginger, nutmeg, and salt. Stir to mix the ingredients evenly. Bring the mixture to a simmer over medium heat. Cover the pan, reduce the heat, and simmer for 10 minutes. Remove the cinnamon stick.

PASS the mixture through a food mill or process in a food processor. Leave the applesauce slightly chunky. Place it in a storage container and let it stand overnight, allowing the flavors to blend. Before serving, warm the applesauce briefly in a microwave oven.

BACON ROAST APPLES

3 Granny Smith apples   9 slices bacon

SLICE each apple into 6 equal sized wedges, and trim the center of each slice to remove the seeds. Cut each slice of bacon in half. Tightly wrap each apple wedge with a bacon slice, securing it with a toothpick. Freeze the apples for at least 2 hours or overnight. (Make the caramel butter and the flipjack batter.)

WHILE the flipjack batter is standing, preheat the oven to 350°F. Place the frozen apples on a baking sheet, and bake for 20 to 25 minutes or until the bacon is crispy and lightly browned. Keep the oven on for the flipjacks.

CARAMEL BUTTER

¼ cup sugar   ¼ cup heavy cream
2 tablespoons water   ¼ pound butter, softened (½ cup)

FOLLOWING the instructions on page 67, form a caramel with the sugar and water, and then "shock" the hot caramel with the cream. Stir with a whisk to combine the mixture completely and to help it cool down quickly. Let it stand until it reaches room temperature, about 20 minutes.

WITH a mixer, whip the butter until it is light and airy. Slowly add the caramel mixture and continue whipping until completely combined. Set aside until ready to serve.

WHOLE WHEAT APPLE FLIPJACKS

4 cups milk   1 teaspoon salt
4 eggs   ¾ teaspoon baking soda
2 tablespoons apple brandy   ½ teaspoon ground cinnamon
2 cups all-purpose flour   4 apples, unpeeled
2 cups whole wheat flour   6 tablespoons butter
2 teaspoons ground nutmeg   3 tablespoons sugar
1½ teaspoons baking powder

WHISK together the milk, eggs, and brandy. In a separate bowl, sift together the flours, nutmeg, baking powder, salt, baking soda, and cinnamon. Form a well in the center of the flour mixture and pour in the milk mixture. With a few quick strokes, combine the wet and dry ingredients until almost completely mixed, leaving the batter slightly lumpy. Let it stand for 30 minutes.

SLICE each apple into 12 wedges that are all the same thickness. (Sixteen wedges will be used to make each of 3 flipjacks.) Remove the seeds.

MELT 2 tablespoons of the butter in a medium, ovenproof skillet, swirling it around to thoroughly coat the bottom of the pan. Sprinkle 1 tablespoon of the sugar evenly onto the butter. Align apple wedges around the outer edge of the pan (on their sides) so that each points toward the center. Make sure that the apple skins are all facing in the same direction. Arrange more apple wedges in a single layer completely covering the bottom of the pan.

PLACE the pan over medium heat until the butter begins to sizzle. Leave the pan on the heat for a few moments until the bottoms of the apples brown slightly. Remove from the heat and pour one-third of the batter over the apples, being careful not to disturb them.

PLACE the pan in the hot oven and bake for 10 to 12 minutes, or until the batter is fully cooked. The flipjack will puff up, and the top will begin to brown and will feel stiff when the flipjack is done.

REMOVE the pan from the oven. With a quick motion, invert the flipjack onto a serving plate, cover, and keep in a warm place until all the flipjacks are cooked. Repeat the process twice with the remaining batter. Reheat the flipjacks briefly in the oven as the last one cooks.

PRESENTATION

(See the color photo illustrating the presentation of this dish.)

CUT each flipjack into 4 wedges. Overlap 2 flipjack wedges on each of 6 warm plates. Pour on some of the applesauce, and arrange 3 of the bacon roast apples on each plate. Finish each serving with a dollop of the caramel butter, or serve it separately.

CHEF'S HINTS

The butter in the bottom of the pan is helpful in caramelizing the sugar and apples, and adds an extra flavor dimension as it gets absorbed by the batter during baking. ✳ Don't hesitate when you are flipping the pan over. If you're wary, try capping the pan first with the plate, then flipping the works.

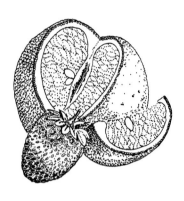

Oatmeal Crusted French Toast with Orange Marmalade Mint Stuffing and Strawberry Sauce

This is a versatile recipe — any fruit jam can be used to stuff the French toast.

6 SERVINGS

Strawberry Sauce

3 cups sliced strawberries
¼ pound butter (½ cup)

½ cup honey
Juice and zest of 1 lemon

PLACE the strawberries, butter, honey, and lemon juice and zest in a small saucepan and bring to a simmer. Pour the mixture into a blender and process until smooth. Set aside.

Oatmeal Crusted French Toast with Orange Marmalade Mint Stuffing

CHEF'S HINT

Many different breads can work in this recipe; choose one that suits your taste. Use an unsliced loaf so you can cut the slices the right thickness. Be careful to make the pockets in the bread slices even and deep, and to distribute the filling evenly.

1 cup cream cheese
1 cup orange marmalade
1 cup mint leaves
2 cups milk
8 eggs

½ cup sugar
1 teaspoon ground cinnamon
6 slices bread, 1 to 1½ inches thick
3 cups large-flake rolled oats
6 tablespoons butter

PREHEAT the oven to 350°F and lightly grease a baking sheet.

IN a food processor, process the cream cheese, marmalade, and mint until smooth.

IN a separate bowl, beat together the milk, eggs, sugar, and cinnamon. Pour the mixture into a shallow pan big enough to hold all the bread slices in 1 layer.

CUT a deep pocket into each bread slice (see drawing), keeping the opening as small as possible. Fill the center of each slice with the cream cheese mixture, and soak the stuffed bread slices in the milk mixture for 20 minutes, turning several times.

PLACE the oatmeal in a bowl, and dredge the bread slices, coating each evenly with the oatmeal.

MELT 2 tablespoons of the butter in a large, nonstick skillet over medium heat. Brown 2 of the bread slices on each side. Repeat. Place the bread slices on the baking sheet and bake, turning once, for 8 to 10 minutes. Serve immediately with strawberry sauce.

MULTIGRAIN GRANOLA WITH CINNAMON CRUSTED WALNUTS AND MAPLE RAISINS

This quick and easy granola recipe can be made ahead for gourmet breakfasts on the fly.

12 CUPS

1 egg white
3 tablespoons packed brown sugar
1 tablespoon ground cinnamon
4 cups walnut halves
½ cup vegetable oil
3 cups large-flake rolled oats
1 cup whole wheat flakes

1 cup sunflower seeds
1 cup unsweetened shredded coconut
½ cup wheat germ
1 teaspoon salt
2 cups raisins
1 cup maple syrup

PREHEAT the oven to 350°F. Lightly oil a double-bottomed baking sheet.

IN a small bowl, vigorously whisk together the egg white, brown sugar, and cinnamon until loose and watery, about 30 seconds. Add the walnuts and stir well until they are thoroughly coated with the egg white mixture. Spread the coated walnuts in an even layer on the baking sheet, and bake for 12 minutes. Remove and let cool for several minutes, then loosen the nuts with a metal spatula. Let the nuts cool completely while the granola is baking.

POUR the vegetable oil into a 13 by 9-inch baking pan. Place the pan in the oven and turn the oven down to 325°F. Heat the pan in the oven for 10 minutes, then stir in the oats and wheat flakes. Bake the grains until they are toasted and golden brown, stirring frequently, about 15 minutes. Stir in the sunflower seeds, coconut, wheat germ, and salt and continue baking until toasted, about another 10 minutes, stirring several times. Prepare the raisins while the granola finishes baking.

PLACE the raisins and maple syrup in a small saucepan on medium heat and bring to a simmer. Simmer for 5 minutes. Stir the hot raisin mixture into the granola when it has finished baking.

WHEN the granola has cooled to room temperature, stir in the walnuts. Store the granola in a sealed container at room temperature for up to 5 days, or for several weeks in the refrigerator.

CHEF'S HINTS

If you don't have a double bottomed baking sheet to bake the walnuts, place the baking sheet on another sheet to insulate the bottom and prevent the walnuts from burning. Watch the granola carefully in the last few minutes of baking.
✳ This recipe can easily be modified by adding a variety of spices, dried fruits, or nuts. Try substituting honey for the maple syrup.

WHOLE GRAIN COUNTRY BREAD

This is our signature bread. Our miller Steve Knechtel — the baking guru of Prince Edward Island — grinds whole wheat flour for us every week.

2 (9 BY 5-INCH) LOAVES

CHEF'S HINT

A good health food store will have a broad selection of grains that can be used in the grain mix for this bread. Some stores may even have a grain mixture available.

2 packages active dry yeast (2 tablespoons)
¼ cup honey
2 cups warm water
4 cups bread flour*
3 cups whole wheat flour
1 cup rye flour

1 cup mixed grains such as flax seed, cracked wheat, or rye
½ cup powdered instant milk
½ cup wheat germ
1 tablespoon salt
½ cup walnut oil

*Bread flour or baker's flour is a high gluten flour available at many supermarkets or specialty food stores.

DISSOLVE the yeast and honey in the water. Let the mixture stand for 10 minutes.

MIX the flours, grains, powdered milk, wheat germ, and salt until thoroughly combined. On a smooth dry surface, make a mound of the flour mixture and form a well in the center. Pour in the yeast mixture and oil. Using your hands, gradually combine the flour mixture with the yeast mixture until a dough is formed. Knead the dough until it is smooth and elastic, about 15 minutes. Cover the dough and let it stand for 30 minutes in a warm place.

GREASE 2 (9 by 5-inch) loaf pans. On a floured surface, knead the dough for a few minutes until the dough shrinks and becomes solid. Divide it into 2 equal pieces. Shape each piece into a loaf and place in a prepared loaf pan. Let the dough rise until it has doubled, about 60 minutes.

PREHEAT the oven to 350°F. Bake the loaves for about 45 minutes. The loaves will have expanded and will be evenly browned when they are done. Remove them from the pans and cool on a rack.

Cornmeal Bread

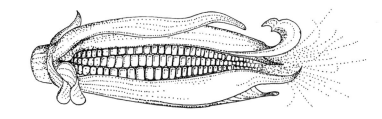

The cornmeal in this bread gives it a very interesting texture and little spots of color. The by-hand method is reminiscent of bread making before electricity — no machines, no tools, no bowls. I enjoy making this bread as much as eating it! It is best toasted.

2 (9 BY 5-INCH) LOAVES

5 cups bread flour
2 cups yellow cornmeal
1 tablespoon salt
2 cups warm water

2 tablespoons sugar
3 packages active dry yeast (3 tablespoons)
¼ pound butter, melted (½ cup)

On a large, smooth, dry surface, make a mound of the flour, cornmeal, and salt. Using your hands, mix the ingredients completely. Form a well in the center of the flour mixture, and pour the water into the well. Sprinkle the sugar and then the yeast evenly over the surface of the water. With a finger, stir the water to dissolve the yeast and sugar. Let the mixture stand until it becomes frothy and bubbly, about 15 minutes.

Pour in the melted butter. With your hands, form a dough by mixing the water and flour mixtures. Start by gradually stirring more and more of the flour into the center of the well until that part becomes a sticky mass. Knead until a dough forms, gradually picking up all of the flour as you work. Continue kneading until the dough is smooth and elastic, about 15 minutes. Let the dough stand, covered, for 15 minutes.

Grease 2 (9 by 5-inch) loaf pans. Divide the dough into 2 equal pieces. Shape each piece into a loaf and place in a prepared loaf pan. Make a ½-inch-deep cut in the loaves lengthwise to within 1 inch in of each end. Let the dough rise until it has doubled, about 60 minutes.

Preheat the oven to 350°F. Bake the loaves for about 45 minutes. Remove them from the pans and cool on a rack.

CHEF'S HINT

To form a well in the flour mixture, push your hands into the center of the mound, pushing back the flour until it forms 4-inch walls around a bare center about 12 inches across. Be careful not to break through the walls as you begin mixing the dough. It will take several minutes of kneading to incorporate all of the flour; be patient. The kneading process will also clean the counter where a crust forms from the wet flour.

BLACK PEPPER YEAST BREAD

The pepper in this bread gives it an unusual savory edge, and, although a bland flour is used, the bread has a strong yeast flavor.

2 (9 BY 5-INCH) LOAVES

CHEF'S HINT

This bread can add a savory touch to many dishes. Use it to make sandwiches or salad croutons. It is also very good toasted and served with a variety of cheeses or pâtés.

2 packages active dry yeast (2 tablespoons)
2 tablespoons sugar
2 cups milk, at room temperature
6½ cups all-purpose flour

2 tablespoons coarsely ground black pepper
1 tablespoon salt
2 tablespoons butter, melted

ADD the yeast and sugar to the milk and stir until dissolved. Let the mixture stand for 10 minutes.

IN a bowl, mix the flour, pepper, and salt until thoroughly combined. On a smooth dry surface, make a mound of the flour mixture and form a well in the center. Pour in the yeast mixture and melted butter. Using your hands, gradually combine the flour mixture with the yeast mixture until a dough is formed. Knead the dough until it is smooth and elastic. Cover the dough and let it stand for 60 minutes in a warm place.

GREASE 2 (9 by 5-inch) loaf pans. On a floured surface, knead the dough for a few minutes until the dough shrinks and becomes solid. Divide it into 2 equal pieces. Shape each piece into a loaf and place in a prepared loaf pan. Let the dough rise until it has doubled, about 60 minutes.

PREHEAT the oven to 350°F. Bake the loaves for about 45 minutes. They will have expanded further and will be lightly browned. Remove them from the pans and cool on a rack.

Chive Biscuits with
Scrambled Egg Stuffing,
Cheddar Sauce, and Bacon
(page 36)

**Whole Wheat
Apple Flipjacks with
My Mom's Applesauce,
Caramel Butter, and
Bacon Roast Apples**
(page 41)

A Malpeque
Oyster Tasting:
Some Hot, Some Cold,
All Different
(page 78)

Smoked Salmon Rye Bread Pudding with
Dill Yogurt Sauce, Dijon Mousse, and
Juniper Pickled Red Onions
(page 89)

WHIPPED BROWN BUTTER

Butter has an amazing nutty flavor when it is browned. This recipe captures that essence in a unique bread spread. To me, it represents the full flavor of butter.

1 1/2 CUPS

3/8 pound butter, softened (3/4 cup)

USING 4 tablespoons of the butter, follow the instructions on page 67 for brown butter. Let it cool to room temperature.

IN a separate bowl, whip the remaining butter until it is light and airy. While still whipping, slowly pour in the brown butter and continue whipping until it is thoroughly incorporated.

CHEF'S HINTS

If you have a pastry bag, pipe the butter into rosettes and store them in the refrigerator until needed. You can also serve the butter in a crock or other decorative container. ✳ Always serve whipped butters at room temperature. ✳ Whipped brown butter can be stored in the refrigerator for 2 weeks.

WHIPPED BUTTER WITH OLIVE OIL

This is a great way to combine two distinctive favorite flavors into a bread spread.

1 1/2 CUPS

3/8 pound butter, softened (3/4 cup)   1/4 cup extra virgin olive oil

PLACE the butter in a bowl and whip at high speed until it is light and airy. Slowly pour the olive oil into the butter, and continue whipping until the oil is thoroughly incorporated. Either place the butter in a serving container or use a pastry bag to pipe it into shapes.

CHEF'S HINTS

Use a strongly flavored, high-quality olive oil, preferably a first cold pressing from a reputable producer. This recipe will highlight the flavor of the oil. ✳ If you chill the whipped butter, it becomes difficult to spread, so be sure to let it come to room temperature before serving it. ✳ This butter can be stored in the refrigerator for 2 weeks.

FAZOOL

This is another spread that we sometimes serve with our breads. Combined with a hearty bread, it can be a meal by itself! The beans must be soaked for eight hours before they are cooked. The name fazool refers to white beans used in Italian cooking.

4 CUPS

1 cup white beans
4 cups water
½ cup chopped onion
¼ cup chopped carrot
2 cloves garlic, chopped

½ tablespoon grated fresh ginger
½ cup extra virgin olive oil
4 tablespoons balsamic vinegar
½ teaspoon salt

SOAK the beans in the water for 8 hours or overnight.

BRING the beans to a simmer in the same water in which they were soaked. Use a pot with a tight fitting lid. Turn the heat to its lowest possible setting. Cover and simmer for 60 minutes.

ADD the onion, carrot, garlic, and ginger. Stir and continue simmering for another 60 minutes. At the end of this period, check the beans to see if they are completely cooked: they should be soft. If they are not, continue to simmer the beans, adding 1 or 2 cups of water if needed. Check the beans every 15 minutes until they are completely cooked. If there is still water in the pot when the beans are tender, turn up the heat and evaporate the water, stirring constantly to prevent burning.

PLACE the beans, oil, vinegar, and salt in a food processor or blender and purée the mixture until it is completely smooth. Place the purée in a serving dish and cool. The fazool may be refrigerated for 1 week.

CHEF'S HINTS

Beans are very inconsistent; some will take much longer to cook than others of the same variety. By presoaking them, you lessen the time they need to cook. ✳ After 2 hours of cooking, watch carefully to be sure that the pot doesn't dry out before the beans are done. It may be necessary to add a little water during the cooking. The object is to have the beans finish cooking just as they absorb the last of the water. ✳ This recipe is a great way to show off your best olive oil, so use a flavorful one. If you prefer, make the fazool richer by adding more olive oil.

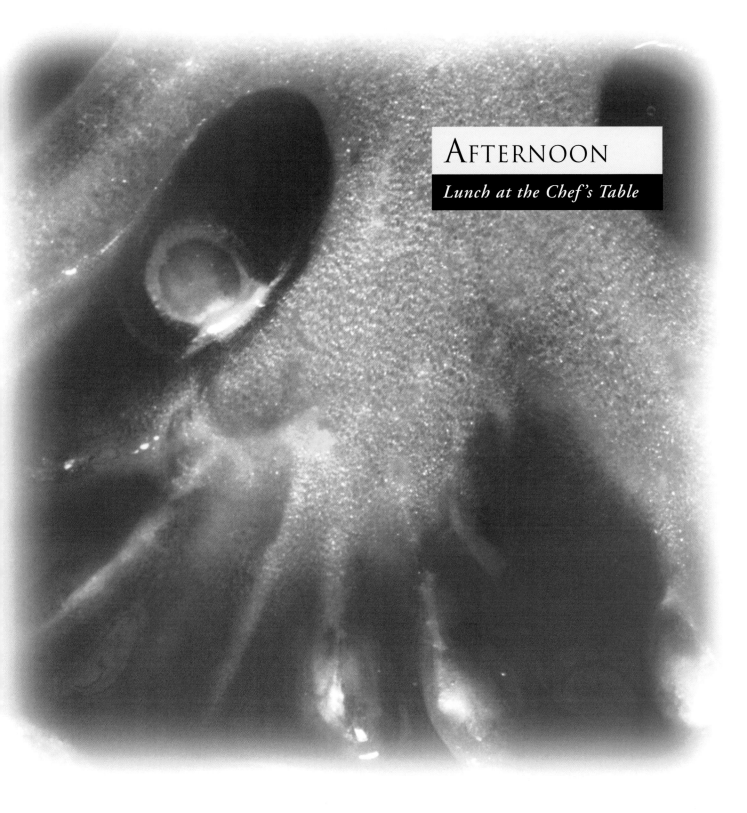

AFTERNOON

Lunch at the Chef's Table

12:45 pm: In the kitchen, the day's work is in full swing. The cooks are busy preparing mise-en-place *for the dinner stations. The chef has returned with the lamb. With one eye on the clock, he is explaining to one of the cooks how the various parts of the animal should be cut. The fish cook is shucking mussels, fresh from the nearby bay where they are aquacultured. The salad cooks are whisking vinaigrettes and preparing muses, the artfully presented morsels with which guests are welcomed at the start of their meal. The phone rings, and, after a quick conversation, the chef announces that a local fisherman is bringing in a thousand-pound bluefin tuna and asks if anyone wants to see the giant fish. As several of the cooks pile into the Jeep for the drive down to the wharf, someone remarks "What's for lunch?"*

In our kitchen, there is rarely time for the staff to stop and enjoy a leisurely meal. What time there is is usually not enough to prepare anything elaborate, so our own meals tend to be relatively simple. Although we are known for our amazing cuisine, many of us are quite content to relax with a bowl of spaghetti.

I encourage my cooks to taste every item on the menu, and they all have the option of dining once a month at no expense. I want them to be aware of the total dining experience at the Inn. The best

Team Cuisine takes a well-deserved break.

way to do that is to sit in the dining room and enjoy the evening the same way a guest would. But no one can enjoy fine dining every day. (Have you ever heard restaurant critics complain about their job?) A lot of very talented cooks have their own version of comfort food.

Over the years, a few dishes have come to define the meals that we professional cooks enjoy. The following recipes are some of our favorites. They are what we eat when no one's looking!

KID'S SAUCE

We call this kid's sauce because it's made just in case any kids decide that our menu is too fancy and request spaghetti. The reality is that the cooks eat far more of it than anyone else!

8 CUPS

½ cup extra virgin olive oil
2 large onions, chopped (about 4 cups)
1 head garlic, peeled and minced
2 (5½-ounce) cans tomato paste
1 cup red wine

3 (19-ounce) cans plum or roma tomatoes
  in juice
1 teaspoon Bay Fortune seasoning (page 66)
1 teaspoon salt

IN a thick-bottomed saucepan, heat the oil over medium heat. Add the onion and cook, stirring frequently, until it begins to turn golden. Reduce the heat and continue cooking and stirring until the onion is a deep, golden brown. Add the garlic and cook for a few minutes more. Add the tomato paste and cook, stirring constantly, for a few minutes more.

ADD the red wine, tomatoes, Bay Fortune seasoning, and salt. Bring the sauce to a simmer, simmer for 20 minutes, and remove from the heat.

PROCESS the sauce in a food processor or pass it through a food mill, leaving the sauce slightly chunky.

CHEF'S HINTS

This sauce is always better the day after it's made. It will go well with your favorite pasta. ✳ If it's summer and you have vine-ripened sauce tomatoes, use them; otherwise stick to canned plum tomatoes. Use a good brand and you will find that they have far more flavor than any fresh ones. Tomatoes bound for the cannery are left on the vine far longer than those that are picked immature for a long truck ride.

| JEFF'S SALSA

Jeff McCourt, our sous-chef, is very proud of his salsa recipe. It's an example of how a great cook pays attention to the details, whatever the preparation. We eat it with simple grilled fish or chicken and, of course, it goes great with chips.

ABOUT 5 CUPS

CHEF'S HINTS

Allowing certain preparations such as this salsa to stand overnight has a dramatically positive effect on the flavor. ✴ If you like a milder salsa, remove the white pith from the jalapeño before mincing it. If you like a spicier salsa, use more jalapeños or your favorite pepper. ✴ The salsa can be stored for several weeks in the refrigerator.

2 cups tomato juice
2 cups finely diced ripe tomatoes
½ cup chopped cilantro
½ cup extra virgin olive oil
½ cup finely diced green pepper
½ cup grated radish

½ cup minced red onion
½ cup peeled, finely diced cucumber
2 large cloves garlic, minced
1 jalapeño, minced
1 teaspoon salt
Juice and zest of 2 limes

REDUCE the tomato juice by half in a small pot over medium heat.

IN a bowl, combine the tomato, cilantro, oil, green pepper, radish, onion, cucumber, garlic, jalapeño, salt, and lime juice and zest. Pour in the tomato juice and mix completely. Refrigerate the salsa overnight.

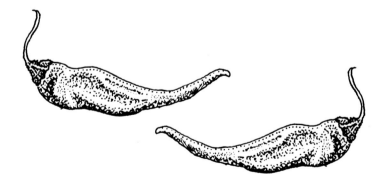

Salad of Grilled New York Sirloin with Mixed Greens, Black Pepper Croutons, Blue Cheese, and Warm Brown Butter Balsamic Vinaigrette

This is my favorite steak dish. Searing the meat in browning butter is a simple method, perfect for when you crave something quick and flavorful.

2 SERVINGS

1 slice black pepper yeast bread (page 48), cut into ½-inch cubes (about 1 cup)
1 tablespoon extra virgin olive oil
6 tablespoons butter
1 New York sirloin steak (about 12 ounces, 1½ inches thick)
4 cloves garlic, minced

2 shallots, minced
3 tablespoons balsamic vinegar
2 tablespoons Dijon mustard
4 handfuls mixed baby greens
1 cup crumbled blue cheese
Black pepper
Coarse grained salt

CHEF'S HINT

The trick to this recipe is not to burn the butter before the steak is cooked. Success requires a careful eye and medium heat. Adjust the heat if the steak is cooking too quickly.

PREHEAT the oven to 400°F.

TOSS the bread cubes in the olive oil. Place them on a baking sheet, and bake until they are toasted and golden brown, about 10 minutes.

IN a nonstick skillet, melt the butter over medium heat. When the butter begins to foam, place the steak in the pan. Sear the steak on both sides, being careful not to burn the butter. Don't shake the pan, and turn the steak only once: constant handling will slow down the searing. Continue searing until the steak reaches the degree of doneness you prefer. (For medium rare, cook it 10 to 12 minutes.) Remove the steak from the pan and invert the steak onto a plate.

SAUTÉ the garlic and shallots briefly in the brown butter left in the pan. Remove the pan from the heat, and add the balsamic vinegar and mustard. Stir until the vinaigrette has a smooth consistency.

CUT the steak across the grain into slices about ¼ inch wide. Toss the slices with the greens, blue cheese, and warm vinaigrette. Top with the croutons. Season with pepper and salt. Serve immediately.

WINE: Medium- to full-bodied dry red wine such as a Merlot or Pomerol.

Reuben Bread Pudding with Maple-Onion Jam

This dish was inspired by my favorite sandwich!

4 SERVINGS

Reuben Bread Pudding

4 slices rye bread, cut into ½-inch cubes (about 4 cups)
1 cup milk
2 tablespoons coarse grained mustard
1 tablespoon Dijon mustard
¼ teaspoon black pepper
¼ teaspoon ground caraway seeds

½ teaspoon salt
2 whole eggs
1 egg yolk
6 ounces cooked corned beef, cut into ½-inch cubes (about 1 cup)
½ cup sauerkraut
¼ cup snipped chives

PREHEAT the oven to 350°F. Grease 4 (8-ounce) ramekins with cooking spray.

PLACE the bread cubes on a baking sheet, and bake 15 to 20 minutes until they are completely toasted and golden brown.

IN a saucepan, heat the milk, mustards, pepper, caraway, and salt until the mixture simmers. Remove from heat.

WHISK the egg and egg yolk together in a large bowl. Slowly add the milk mixture and whisk to combine. Add the bread cubes, corned beef, sauerkraut, and chives, and combine. Let stand 20 minutes.

BRING a kettle of water to the boil.

DIVIDE the batter among the ramekins. Place them in a pan and fill it with the hot water to two-thirds the depth of the pudding. Bake about 45 minutes until the edges of the puddings pull away from the ramekins and the pudding centers are set.

Maple-Onion Jam

1 large onion, sliced
2 tablespoons extra virgin olive oil

½ cup maple syrup
¼ teaspoon salt

In a skillet, cook the onion slowly in the oil, stirring frequently, until the onion is caramelized to a deep, golden brown. As it cooks, gradually lower the heat to avoid burning the onion. (This step takes patience!) When the onion is brown, add the maple syrup and simmer for 5 minutes. Remove from heat, and season with the salt.

Presentation

Unmold the puddings onto 4 warm plates and serve with warm maple-onion jam.

CHEF'S HINTS

This jam can be made ahead and refrigerated. It's also great served cold as a condiment. ✳ Try adding some coarse grained mustard with the maple syrup.

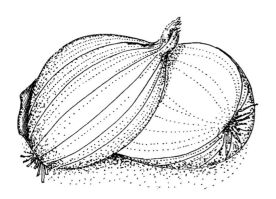

Slow Baked Chicken with Lemon, Thyme, Root Vegetables, and Whole Garlic

This is the way I cook at home: simply. This method is a snap and the cleanup is easy (on my day off I don't want to be in the kitchen!). The long, slow baking of the chicken tenderizes it and gives it a wonderful aroma, and the resulting broth is perfect for dipping crusty French bread into.

4 SERVINGS

CHEF'S HINTS

The chicken and vegetables should fit in the casserole without a great deal of remaining space. At home, I use a large enameled cast-iron casserole; its thick walls slowly radiate the heat that bakes the chicken. ✳ This recipe is infinitely variable: try modifying it with any herb, chilies, spices, or other vegetables. ✳ Serve this dish in large bowls to hold the delicious broth.

1 fryer chicken (about 5 pounds)
2 lemons
8 thyme sprigs
1 tablespoon extra virgin olive oil
2 teaspoons salt
Black pepper

3 medium carrots, diced (about 2 cups)
2 heads garlic, peeled
1 medium celery root, diced (about 2 cups)
1 large onion, diced (about 2 cups)
1 cup Chardonnay

PREHEAT the oven to 300°F.

RINSE the chicken well in water and pat dry. Cut the lemons in half and place them in the chicken cavity with 4 of the thyme sprigs.

REMOVE the leaves from 2 of the thyme sprigs. Combine the oil with 1 teaspoon of the salt, some pepper, and the thyme leaves. Rub the chicken with the oil mixture.

FROM the remaining thyme sprigs, remove the leaves and mix them with the remaining salt, some more pepper, and the carrot, garlic, celery root, and onion. Place the vegetables in a 6-quart casserole with a tight fitting lid. Pour in the wine. Place the chicken on the vegetables and cover.

BAKE for 2½ hours. Serve immediately.

WINE: Medium- to full-bodied dry white wine such as oak aged Chardonnay or Côte d'Or.

MIKE'S PASTA DU JOUR

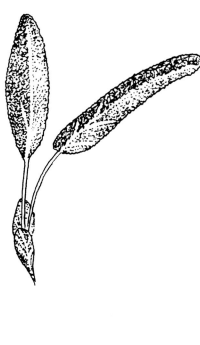

One of the sous-chefs at the Inn, Michael Long, was known for making pasta dishes in minutes from whatever ingredients he happened to find. He now has his own very successful restaurant in Florida. This dish remains one of my favorites.

4 SERVINGS

1 pound dried fettuccine
½ cup cubed pancetta bacon
¼ cup extra virgin olive oil
¼ cup minced shallot
4 large cloves garlic, thinly sliced
24 large shrimp, heads left on
2 cups Chardonnay

4 cups heavy cream
2 red peppers, roasted and sliced (about 1 cup)
1 tablespoon hot red pepper flakes
2 cups grated Asiago cheese
3 tablespoons thinly sliced sage
1 teaspoon salt

BRING a large pot of salted water to the boil. Add the fettuccine and begin cooking it. (The total cooking time should be about 10 minutes, during which the sauce is made.)

IN a large sauté pan over high heat, crisp the pancetta in the oil. Add the shallot and garlic and sauté briefly. Add the shrimp and sauté for several minutes until just done. Add the wine and reduce it quickly to glaze the shrimp. Remove the shrimp and set it aside as you continue reducing the wine.

ADD the cream, roasted pepper, and pepper flakes. Reduce the liquid by half (about 3 to 5 minutes), then add the cheese, sage, and salt. Stir the ingredients together to form a sauce. Add the shrimp and heat it through.

FINISH cooking the fettuccine. Without rinsing it, strain the fettuccine, divide it evenly among 4 large pasta bowls. Pour the sauce over the fettuccine, arrange the shrimp in each bowl, and serve immediately.

WINE: Medium- to full-bodied dry white wine such as Italy's Orvietto Classico.

CHEF'S HINTS

A large, hot pan is needed for this method so that the shrimp will cook quickly.
✳ The sauce can be made in the time that the fettuccine cooks if the ingredients are ready and the pan is very hot. ✳ Don't rinse the pasta: the starch that adheres to it after cooking will blend with the sauce, helping to coat each strand evenly.

GINGER ROSE HIP ICED TEA

This is a true iced tea: its potent flavors are meant to be diluted by ice as it is sipped. When well chilled, this tea is one of the favorite afternoon beverages at the Inn.

2 QUARTS

CHEF'S HINTS

The tea in tea bags is ground or chopped very fine, and loses flavor rapidly unless stored in an airtight container. ✳ Try using your favorite herbal tea in this recipe.

2 quarts water
1 cup sugar
Juice and zest of 4 lemons
2 tablespoons grated fresh ginger
2 tablespoons rose hips*

1 cup mint leaves
12 teaspoons black tea such as Darjeeling (or 12 tea bags)
Lemon wedges
Mint sprigs

*Rose hips, the fruit of a rose bush that remain after the blossoms are gone, are available in specialty stores.

BRING the water and sugar to the boil in a saucepan. Add the lemon juice and zest, the ginger, and the rose hips, and simmer for several minutes. Remove from the heat and add the mint leaves and tea. Cover the pot and let it stand for 10 minutes.

STRAIN the tea mixture through a fine mesh strainer. Place in a storage container and refrigerate until chilled, about 2 hours.

SERVE the tea over ice with a lemon wedge and a mint sprig.

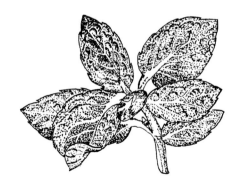

The Chef's Kitchen
(Equipment, Ingredients, and Methods)

1:50 pm: As the chef escorts some guests through the swinging doors into the kitchen, musical chaos greets them. Various cooks are keeping time to the rock and roll rhythm that punctuates afternoon prep time. Every square inch of space is occupied by an intent Team Cuisine member doing a number of tasks almost simultaneously. On the hot side, the fastest paced part of the kitchen, Jeff is demonstrating the intricacies of a difficult butchering method to one of the apprentice cooks. Norman, the first cook, keeps an eye on simmering lamb shanks as he speeds through a potato peeling duel with a prep cook. The stove is full, every burner occupied by a preparation under Norman's watchful eye. The ovens are crammed. Full baking sheets are lined up near them, on hold until oven space is available.

About two hundred individual components are needed for the menu every evening. To prepare for the evening rush, the making of each item must be organized efficiently. At each station, the staff are referring to a prep list that outlines what is needed. The chef confers briefly with one of the cold side cooks, who is forming cookie cups for one of the desserts. The previous evening, orders exceeded prepared cookie cups, and the cold side staff was embarrassed to have to make more in the middle of the dinner period. The chef is reassured that the event will not be repeated. As the guests make their way to the kitchen's back door to see the garden, they can see the balance of brute force and delicacy needed to prepare for the evening's meals.

Balancing the demands of an intricate menu with the desire to serve freshly prepared food is one of the most challenging aspects of running a restaurant kitchen. A successful chef is an expert at predicting the volume of orders that a certain menu item will inspire. The menu is analyzed, and those items that can be are prepared in advance. What these are, of course, depends on the restaurant's style of food. In many restaurants, everything is completely prepared before the guest receives a menu. Orders are filled instantly with precooked vegetables, sauce, and the main item, as well as pre-plated salad and dessert.

At the Inn, however, we practice a style of cooking known as *à la minute:* the cooking of the main components of a meal begins only after an order is received. All meat is grilled to order, every fish is cooked moments before being served, and vegetables are freshly prepared. When every element is perfect, the plates are artfully arranged and whisked steaming to the dining room.

Of course, it would be impossible to make a potato purée every time it was ordered, or begin a three-hour braising of lamb shanks at dinnertime. Therefore, our *à la minute* methods must blend seamlessly with the preparations of the afternoon. The afternoon is spent picking, cleaning, trimming, and cutting the garden's harvest. Meat is cut, and fish is scaled. Cold sauces are made for the desserts and first courses, vinaigrettes are whisked, and cream is whipped. Hot sauces are simmered, seasoned, and strained, ready for careful reheating when required. Some of the more elaborate vegetable preparations are preassembled.

The harvest from the Inn's garden.

Even in the finest restaurants, of necessity many tasks are started well in advance of the dinner period. Careful finishing methods characterize the best kitchens. A fresh tomato purée, heated only when needed, will maintain its essence in a way that cannot be achieved when it is kept hot for a long time. A perfectly baked tart warmed briefly before serving, or a chowder base heated only when ordered, are further examples of our method. Many of the recipes in this book, however, actually benefit from being prepared ahead, some by as much as 24 hours.

During any given day at the Inn, a vast array of equipment, ingredients, and methods is used. The following sections describe some that are especially useful in the home kitchen.

Equipment

Blender

Only a blender achieves the purées needed to finish many of the sauces and other preparations in my kitchen. A food processor does not produce the same quality. These purées must be absolutely smooth to give the most pleasing mouthfeel. A blender also makes great margaritas!

Citrus Zester

This tool is indispensable for capturing the essence of citrus fruit, which is present in the oil of the peel. Citrus zest is packed with flavor. A zester is an inexpensive hand-held device that employs a series of small, sharp-edged holes to slice thin strips of the outer peel without digging into the underlying bitter pith. It takes a bit of practice to master this gadget, but the results are well worth it. Try holding the zester stationary with one hand while turning the fruit with the other. At the Inn, when a cook is instructed to add a lemon to a preparation, he or she understands that both the juice and the zest should be added.

Fine Mesh Strainer

This is the ultimate finishing tool for adding polish to your cooking. Unlike other strainers that allow larger particles through, nothing

Within reach — a tool for every job.

other than the essence of a sauce or purée can make it through this strainer. Its tightly woven fine mesh forms a cone shape and is supported by an exterior frame. While it is quite a bit more expensive than ordinary strainers, the expense is justified. My blender and my fine mesh strainer are a gadget team that produces smooth, vegetable-thickened, fat-free sauces with the mouthfeel of rich cream.

Microwave Oven

Technology has made the world of today's chefs far better than that of their predecessors. Before the microwave oven, there was no tool for cooking vegetables quickly and consistently without any fat or loss of flavor. At the Inn, I am happy to show off the microwaves that we use to cook many of our vegetables or to reheat some of our more elaborate vegetable preparations. Of course, we never heat or cook meats or fish in these ovens: they are not suitable for that area of our cuisine. For the purposes I've mentioned, however, I wholeheartedly recommend microwave ovens. I've never seen a professional kitchen that didn't have at least one in use, although I have seen panicked cooks ruining meat in them.

Nonstick Pan

Much of the fat used by chefs is used for a purely mechanical reason — it acts as a lubricant to facilitate cooking in regular cookware. Nonstick pans require very little fat and so have become an integral part of healthy cooking. Why, then, do many of the recipes in this book call for fat even when nonstick pans are used? The simple answer is flavor. To properly sear or brown many of the ingredients in my cuisine it is necessary to use fat.

Nonstick pans have other good qualities: they easily release the browned bits of protein that may form a flavor base for a sauce, and they make cleanup a breeze. It is possible to properly season and care for an ordinary pan so that it functions in much the same way as a nonstick pan. The French were turning out perfect omelets long before Teflon was invented, but even they recognize that modern technology has its benefits. Get some nonstick pans — be a modern cook!

OUNCE SCALE

Many recipes made in the Inn's kitchen require the level of accuracy that can be achieved only when the ingredients are weighed. Some, particularly pastry and baked goods recipes, are simply ratios of weighed ingredients. In the home kitchen, an ounce scale is a useful tool.

PEPPER GRINDER

Freshly ground pepper has an unmistakable perfume that is often missing when preground pepper is used. The pepper in your spice jar could have been ground years ago and thousands of miles away. To take advantage of the full flavor of whole peppercorns, use a peppermill. Use your own culinary judgment when adding fresh pepper; you may prefer more or less than the recipes call for.

A chef's tools are his or her toys.

SPICE GRINDER

Dried herbs and spices possess a wide range of flavors ranging from subtle to bold. They can add an unmistakable character or mysterious nuances to your cuisine.

Spices, however, must be treated as carefully as other ingredients. Don't be fooled: as they occupy a shelf somewhere in your kitchen, they are losing freshness by the moment. At the Inn, we use a vast range of spices in our cuisine. Each is purchased in its whole form from a good supplier. At the moment a spice is needed, we grind it in a standard electric coffee grinder. These grinders are available at any good housewares store and will change the way you think about spices.

SQUEEZE BOTTLES

Have you ever wondered how clever chefs make such alluring patterns of sauces and purées on the plates? The secret is the common squeeze bottle, which has become a fixture in professional kitchens around the globe. By putting your sauce into a squeeze bottle, you can add flair to your presentation of food. Many kitchen stores now stock squeeze bottles, as do companies that supply beauty products. You can also use ketchup or mustard squeeze bottles, when they have been emptied.

TASTING SPOONS

At the Inn, every station in the kitchen has a small container of spoons standing by, ready to use for tasting. Get in the habit of doing the same in your kitchen. Taste everything you cook, at each step in its preparation. Use a spoon, not your fingers.

INGREDIENTS

ALLSPICE PEPPER

Very often I combine whole allspice with whole black peppercorns to create a deliciously scented blend of the two spices. Allspice has a distinctive, pepperlike aroma with elements of clove and cinnamon, and accentuates the highly aromatic, often overlooked qualities of the peppercorn. When freshly ground together, pepper and allspice are remarkably complementary.

Simply combine three parts whole black peppercorns with one part whole allspice. Place the mixture in a peppermill, and use it wherever you normally use freshly ground black pepper.

BAY FORTUNE SEASONING

Every cuisine has a distinctive spice or flavor mix that characterizes it. The French have the ubiquitous *fines herbes* (mixed herbs) and *mirepoix* (onion, carrot, and celery). In India, intricate curry recipes are passed from one generation to another. Chinese five-spice is a distinctive blend of native spices, the Southwest's chili powder is a core flavor of the culture, and no self-respecting Creole cook can survive without the "holy trinity" of green peppers, celery, and onions. Italian cuisine has its own trio — tomato, garlic, and basil — immortalized in the colors of the country's flag! Bay Fortune seasoning was in use in my kitchen long before being recognized as a distinctive element. I used bay laurel leaves often, mainly because of the influence of the various chefs that I have worked with. Over time, I began to accent my stocks, broths, sauces, and recipes with other spices as well. Coriander's peppery citrus flavor and fennel seed's licorice notes became favorites as I began evolving my own spice blends. One day I noticed that in some of my preparations I was relying increasingly on a common set of spices. I codified it, and Bay Fortune seasoning was born!

Seasonings play an important role.

Bay Fortune seasoning is a blend of whole bay laurel leaf, coriander seed, and fennel seed. Each of these has a distinctive taste and aroma that complements those of its partners. The blend is not used as a main flavor, but instead provides complexity to my cuisine. It is used in preparations in which further cooking allows the blend's aromatic qualities to permeate. In that regard, it is very similar to the bay leaf from which it evolved — distinctive, but familiar at the same time.

To make Bay Fortune seasoning, simply combine equal parts, by weight, of whole dried bay laurel leaf, coriander seed, and fennel seed. Grind them together in a spice grinder, and store the powder in an airtight, opaque container, as light will damage the delicate nature of the blend. Use a pinch of Bay Fortune seasoning whenever a recipe in another book calls for bay leaf.

BROWN BUTTER

Many of the recipes in this book call for brown butter. Its essence depends on the carmelization of the sugars in the milk solids present in butter. When butter is browned in a controlled manner, the results are spectacular. Use the following method when brown butter is called for in the recipes.

Place the butter in a high-sided saucepan. Over medium heat, melt the butter. Leave it on the heat as it simmers and begins to foam, and the water present in it evaporates. The foam will rise and subside. Watch carefully as the butter begins to foam once again. During the second foaming, the butter will begin to brown. Swirl it around and watch the color change. Let the butter become a deep, golden brown. It will smell like roasting nuts. At the last second, before the solids in the bottom of the saucepan begin to burn, pour the butter into a bowl to stop the cooking process. Scrape out all of the solids that may be at the bottom of the saucepan. Swirl the butter around to help it cool, and allow it to stand until it reaches room temperature.

The foaming of the butter is an important visual clue. During the second foaming, watch carefully because the butter can scorch in seconds. You may have to sacrifice some butter to master this process, but it will be worth it. Don't discard the brown grit at the bottom of the pot — it's the best part. Serve browned butter with baked potatoes, and you'll quickly understand its allure.

CARAMEL

Caramel is one of the most fascinating culinary creations. By simply heating sugar in a controlled manner, it is possible to unlock a veritable treasure-trove of flavor nuances. Sugars of all kinds can be caramelized. The golden brown skin of a perfectly roasted chicken and the crust of a loaf of bread are the evidence, as in both a form of sugar is present. At the molecular level, sugars undergo complex changes as they caramelize, a process that adds great depth to the flavor of the preparation. Neutrally flavored plain sugar becomes highly flavored tanned caramel!

When a recipe in this book calls for caramel, use the following method. Measure enough water to equal half the amount of sugar called for in the recipe. Place the sugar and water in a medium sized, high-sided saucepan that will hold all the ingredients that are to be combined with the caramel with room to spare. Swirl the mixture around until the sugar is dissolved. Use a moist pastry brush to wipe any sugar crystals clinging to the sides of the pot down into the liquid. Bring the mixture to a boil, and let it simmer until the water is completely evaporated and a sugar syrup is left. Do not stir it or shake the pan. Watch carefully as the temperature of the syrup rises; wait for it to begin changing color. When it is a deep, golden brown, quickly remove the pan from the heat and carefully add the other ingredients called for in the recipe. This will "shock" the caramel, preventing further browning. Be careful: the sugar is very hot! Remove the pan from the heat and let the caramel mixture stand for a few minutes until it relaxes.

CHIVE OIL

This method captures the essence of chives' flavor in a brilliant green oil. At the Inn, chive oil is our equivalent of the ubiquitous parsley sprig so common in many restaurants. The difference, of course, is that we use it with care to add a flavor and color boost to many of our dishes. The herbal pungency of chives melds easily with a wide variety of other ingredients, making this oil a star member of the cast!

Keep a small amount of chive oil on hand in a squeeze bottle. You'll find that it adds a splash of elegance to any savory presentation.

To make chive oil, use a scale to weigh several ounces of coarsely chopped fresh chives. If you are not able to find chives, you may substitute the tops of green onions or even leeks. Weigh out an amount of olive oil equal to twice the weight of the chives. In a blender, process the oil and chives until the mixture is completely smooth. Pour it into a saucepan and begin warming it over high heat. After a few minutes, the mixture will begin to darken in color, and the chives will begin to form distinct clumps and separate from the oil. Continue heating until the mixture begins to bubble. Cook for 2 to 3 minutes longer, then turn off the heat. Pour the mixture into a fine mesh strainer and let it drain without disturbing it. If you don't have a fine mesh strainer, use several layers of cheesecloth instead. When thoroughly drained, pour the oil into a squeeze bottle, avoiding any water that may be present underneath the oil. If necessary, freeze the whole mixture and remove the frozen water later. Refrigerate the oil and use it before its color fades, within about 2 weeks. It may also be frozen for several months.

ROAST CHICKEN BROTH

The meat that we serve at the Inn is purchased on the bone, and in many cases the entire animal is used. This allows us to create a broth from the bones and scraps that remain after butchering. The meat scraps in a broth distinguish it from stock, which is made from bones only. We always serve broth with the meat from which it is made, usually as the base for an intensely flavored sauce. In a home kitchen, it would be impractical to be so precise, so I recommend the use of chicken broth in many of the recipes in this book. The broth described here is distinguished by the deep flavor that results from the roasting of the bones used to make it, elevating it from a pale neutral liquid to a hearty flavorful broth.

Place 5 pounds of chicken parts such as backs, necks, wings, legs, or thighs in a roasting pan with 2 chopped onions, 2 chopped carrots, and 2 chopped celery stalks. Add 2 cups water. Roast the chicken and vegetables at 425°F for about 1 hour, stirring frequently to promote even browning. When the ingredients are golden brown and caramelized, place them in a stock pot with enough water to cover them. Pour some water into the roasting pan, stir to loosen the browned bits left there, and pour this water into the stock pot. Simmer the broth for 3 hours, skimming off any foamy residue that rises to the top. It is helpful to place the pot so that the burner is underneath only one edge of it. The resulting convection currents will cause the residue to collect on the surface away from the heat, making it easier to remove. After 1 hour or so, when no more residue rises to the top, add 1 teaspoon of Bay Fortune seasoning and continue

Ladles for a variety of sauces.

simmering for about 2 more hours. Strain the broth and refrigerate until needed. It can be stored for 1 week in the refrigerator or for several months in the freezer. When you are ready to use the stock, remove the fat that has congealed on top.

SPRAY OIL

Aerosol spray cans of oil can dramatically lower the amount of fat used in many recipes. Use them when the oil is needed for merely mechanical reasons, such as to lubricate a pan or keep something from sticking. Spray oil is quick and easy and an indispensible part of our nutritional focus at the Inn.

METHODS

ROASTING MEAT

Roasting meat is one of the most common cooking methods employed in kitchens, but it is one that is often poorly understood. The following points are critical to successful roasting.

* To develop flavor, meat is seared before being roasted. Searing does not, never has, and never will seal in the juices. This is a too popular misconception. A variety of methods are employed to sear meat, but all of them should be devoted to building flavor.

* Marinades do not tenderize large pieces of meat. A marinade cannot penetrate to the center of a large roast, or even a small steak, in the time usually allotted. Marinades are used to add flavor. If a piece of meat is left in a vinegar-based marinade long enough, the marinade will penetrate to the center and tenderize it. It will also render the outside mushy and inedible, as well as create a safety hazard due to the length of time needed.

* Pat the meat dry before starting the searing process. The juices that cling to the outside will inhibit the searing.

* Preheat the pan or oven thoroughly before adding the meat to be seared. Searing dries out the meat in order to work. If placed in a cool pan or oven, the meat will cook far more than is necessary before a seared exterior is achieved. The searing process must happen quickly. For this reason, it is often advisable to sear cold meat. Doing so sears the outside without affecting the interior meat.

* Never, ever, salt meat before cooking it. The salt will draw moisture out of the meat and make it dry. Wait until just before serving to season meat with salt. It is a great idea, however, to rub the meat with pepper or other spices.

* Never put meat directly on a flat surface. Doing so allows the juices to flow out of the meat. This is especially true when roasting without a rack: much of the flavor of the meat will be lost to a crust in the pan. Do not put the meat on a flat surface until the meat is served.

* The lower the cooking temperature, the less meat shrinks. High heat creates tension in meat, causing shrinkage that can literally squeeze moisture out of the meat. Low heat produces less of this effect.

* Check the meat for doneness by squeezing or poking it. Don't be tentative — prod it firmly, gauge its feel. It becomes progressively more tense as it cooks. Compare its feel when raw to when it is removed from the oven. With practice, you can develop the ability that chefs have to know the doneness of meat just by touching it.

* Allow the meat to stand before cutting or slicing it. As the meat roasts, the intense outer heat agitates the interior water, driving it to the center. If you cut a steak or roast while it is still very hot, the juice will explode out of it as you release the interior pressure. When meat is left to stand, the water is redistributed throughout the meat, thereby minimizing the amount of juice that flows out of the meat when it is cut. Feel the meat when it is first done cooking, then again after it has been standing for a few minutes. Big difference!

Today's Menus

3:35 pm: The kitchen is still. On the front lawn, the cooks are throwing a Frisbee around, enjoying a break before the evening rush starts. The Inn is full and the phone has been ringing steadily all day. A busy evening is expected. The chef is greeting guests at the front desk when he spots an unexpected pickup truck turning up the lane. By the time the truck stops at the back door, the chef is there to greet the driver. The first chanterelles of the season have arrived, 10 days earlier than expected! As the chef checks out the forager's haul, he remarks, "We haven't even been looking for these ourselves. The season's early this year!" A deal is struck, and the evening's menus will be changed to reflect the unexpected bounty.

The single most defining characteristic of a restaurant is its menu. The menu sets a tone and establishes a tempo, and contributes greatly to the guest's experience of the restaurant's hospitality. Many factors — from the style of service, the wine list, and the music played to the skill of the kitchen staff, the layout and equipment of the kitchen, and the marketing of the restaurant itself — are related to the menu. All of these components contribute to the cohesiveness of the overall picture.

Our menu is not just a random collection of dishes. It is a flexible system that changes daily to reflect the progression of the seasons, allowing fresh mushrooms to make an appearance hours after they arrive at the restaurant. I offer my guests a broad variety of choices, each compelling in its own way. The result is a remarkable diversity of menu items over the course of the season. This evolution of the menu is part of our commitment to excellence.

In devising a menu item, perhaps my primary goal is to be unique. I want guests of the Inn to experience cuisine that is unavailable elsewhere. To a large extent, that goal is achieved by virtue of our location, staff, and ingredients, but the rest is up to me. While classical food is a necessary culinary foundation, we never serve purely classical dishes. We don't copy other chefs' efforts by duplicating their signature dishes; to do so is a form of culinary plagiarism. We also don't use radical flavor combinations solely to be different. But we do strive for a distinctive cuisine that will be memorable to our guests.

Also important to the menu are the nutritional characteristics of the food we serve. Even though ours is a special occasion restaurant where guests indulge their culinary

**North Side Scallops and
South Side Clam Chowder with
an In-Between Potato Crab Cake
(page 102)**

**Campfire Style Rainbow Trout
with Roast Potato Tarragon Salad
and Pickled Rhubarb**
(page 109)

Roast Garlic Stuffed Breast of Chicken with Crisp Corn Pudding and Rosemary Vanilla Jus
(page 112)

**Rye Crusted Lamb Shank
with Scotch Lentil Broth
and Chanterelle Mushrooms**
(page 119)

desires, our menus are carefully restrained, and we use methods designed to promote healthy dining. Since the Inn is a highly regarded dining destination, I feel a responsibility to demonstrate that contemporary cuisine can be good for you.

Deciding what to order can be difficult for some guests. On a menu, everything looks appealing, and guests may feel they will miss something by choosing one dish over another.

Our most popular dining options are the special multicourse Chef's Tasting Menus we offer every day. Each of these menus is a complete progression of courses that complement each other and allow the guest to try far more of our preparations at one meal than would a conventional menu. There are four Chef's Tasting Menus, each with a distinctive theme, that change daily and feature the best ingredients and the unique preparations of our kitchen. "From Our Kitchen Gardens," a menu based on vegetables, is a celebration of our gardens. "From Island Waters" showcases the vast diversity of foods from our maritime environment. "From Island Farms" highlights the agricultural and wild bounty of Prince Edward Island. The "Open Kitchen Tasting" — often served in the kitchen at our special chef's table — is our grand menu for special occasions. The guests join me in the kitchen to customize a menu that constitutes a culinary tour of the island and all that it provides.

One of the characteristics needed to be a successful restaurant is consistency. Consistency is a relative concept at The Inn at Bay Fortune. My presence, of course, is a consistent influence. In that regard, the menu is meant to reflect my participation in the preparation of every plate that leaves the kitchen. In many regards, we try to make the dining experience the same for every guest: this applies to the manner in which they are greeted, to the way they are served, and even to the way wine bottles are opened. In the kitchen, however, artistic expression is paramount. I don't hire or train mindless robots. I expect my cooks to be commited to the culinary process. This commitment may be manifested in trying new ways of executing a dish, adjusting its nuances, or changing its presentation. Often we present the same dish in different ways when several guests at a single table have ordered it.

The style I use when writing a menu is very specific. I avoid culinary terms that most guests won't understand, such as *chiffonade* or *julienne*. These are words for the kitchen staff to use, not for the wait staff to have to explain. I always identify the major components of the dish, including the dominant flavors and cooking methods, because it is important to give guests the correct expectations of a menu item. I never describe the presentation of the food, preferring instead to retain an element of surprise for the guests to enjoy when their meal arrives. *On a bed of* or *lightly sauced with* are irrelevant phrases to me. The words used in the menu can have a dramatic effect on the sale of a dish: obviously anything *fried* is not appealing, while anything *braised* is sure to be a winner. Menus that state *cooked to your satisfaction* amuse me. Satisfaction is implicit when you're asking people to pay for something.

Our menu is conceived with the expectation that wine will be enjoyed with dinner. Our extensive wine list represents the efforts of innkeeper David Wilmer to enhance our kitchen's cooking with wines that highlight the flavor nuances that we strive for. It is our goal to serve all guests wine with their dinner. Our list includes a wide variety of great wines, many of which are available by the glass. Often guests ask me to recommend wines to accompany their meals, and we pair wines with each of the courses of our Chef's Tasting Menus. Food and wine are co-stars in the nightly production.

5:00 pm: It's time for lineup. As the entire evening staff assembles in the kitchen for this quick strategy session, their confidence is apparent. The dining room has been detailed — the menus readied, the glasses shined, the silverware polished, the napkins folded, and the flowers arranged. Team Cuisine is set. A just-prepared menu example is tasted as the chef describes one of the evening's new dishes. "I want the simple pureness of the salmon's flavor to be contrasted by the aggressive watercress. Any of our full-bodied Chardonnays will work here." The innkeeper conducts a tasting, describing the pedigree of a new wine, a Canadian ice wine. "It's world class," he says to the wait staff. A discussion of a problematic service nuance follows and a solution is agreed upon. Everyone is focused on his or her role in the coming drama. "Open kitchen," declares the chef, and the staff head for their posts.

·TODAY'S MENU·
·FIRST·COURSES·

◦ A Malpeque Oyster Tasting: Some Hot, Some Cold, All Different...
◦ Island Blue Mussel and Sweet Potato Chowder with Spicy Butter Swirls...
◦ Caramel and Horseradish Apple Soups with Sharp Cheddar Fritters and Spicy Apple Chutney...
◦ Strawberry Gazpacho with Strawberry Salsa, Black Pepper Croutons and Balsamic Vinegar...
◦ Smoked Salmon Rye Bread Pudding with Dill Yogurt Sauce, Dijon Mousse and Juniper Pickled Red Onions...
◦ Potato, Bacon and Cheddar Tart with Horseradish Broth and Spinach...

·MAIN·COURSES·

◦ North Side Scallops and South Side Clam Chowder with an In-Between Potato Crab Cake...
◦ Blue Cheese Crusted Beef Tenderloin with Brown Butter Potatoes, Asparagus and Cabernet Sauvignon Sauce...
◦ Spice Rubbed Tuna Loin with Saffron Ratatouille, Tomato Anchovy Sauce and Swiss Chard...
◦ Bacon Roast Loin of Pork with a Sweet Potato Pecan Wedge, Sage Peach Chutney and Bourbon Gravy...
◦ Campfire Style Rainbow Trout with Roast Potato Tarragon Salad and Pickled Rhubarb...
◦ Roast Garlic Stuffed Breast of Chicken with Crisp Corn Pudding and Rosemary Vanilla Broth...
◦ Slow Baked Salmon with Horseradish Salsa, Roast Carrot Sauce and a Salad of Pickled Carrots, Cucumber and Watercress...
◦ Rye Crusted Lamb Shank with Scotch Lentil Broth and Chanterelle Mushrooms...
◦ Sautéed Lobster with Pea Pancakes, Pea Shoots and Leeks in Cinnamon Basil Broth...
◦ Pan Seared Skate Wing with Mint Tapenade and Roast Shallot Custard in Tomato, Chive and Caper Water...

·LAST·COURSES·

◦ Cashew Rhubarb Tart with Rosemary Ice Cream and Raspberry Port Sauce...
◦ A Time for Chocolate: Molten Bittersweet Chocolate Cake with Cookie Clock Hands, Spiced Bananas and Rum Froth...
◦ Roasted Carrot Cake with Cream Cheese Sauce, Carrot Ice and Minted Carrots in Riesling Syrup...
◦ Star Anise Chocolate Tart with Pistachios and Sambuca and Mint Soaked Grapefruits...
◦ Seasonal Berry Compote in a Crisp Cookie Cup with Chardonnay Ice and Lemonade Sauce...
◦ Walnut Crusted Blue Cheese Cake with Port Sauce and Pear Mint Chutney...

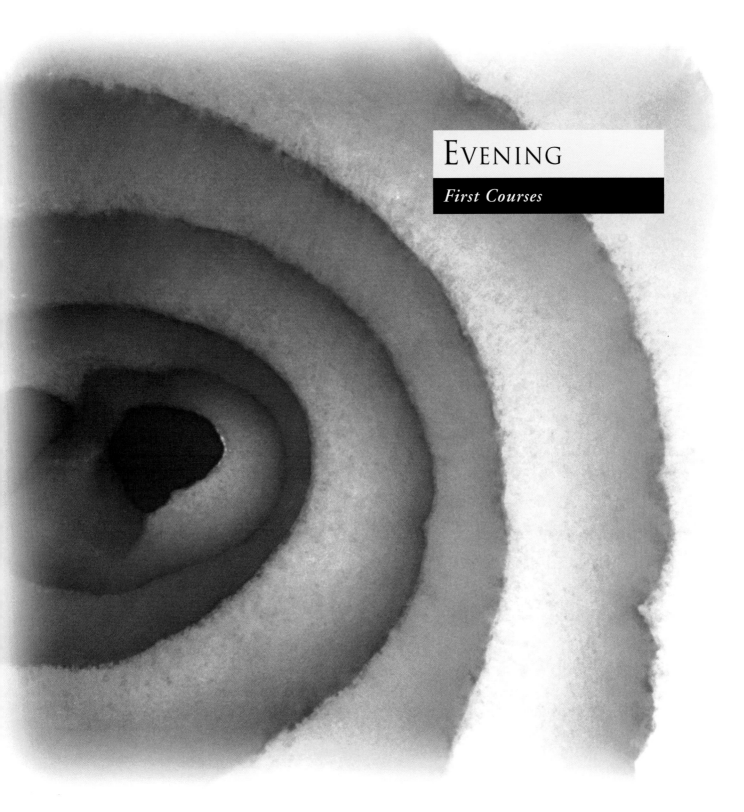

EVENING
First Courses

8:05 pm: It is the height of the evening rush. In the dining room, every table is full. Some guests are reading menus or waiting for their meals, while others are already dining. The wait staff are moving from table to table, unobtrusively executing their precision hospitality. Unbeknown to the guests, each table has an assigned number, which allows the wait staff to communicate with one another and the kitchen staff about the progress of each table's meals. At table 7, a couple has just finished their first courses; the empty plates are whisked away by the server, Bonnie. "Fire table 7," she says as she enters the kitchen. "Fire table 7," echoes the chef as he updates the expeditor's board, moving the table's ticket from one section to another to signify a new status. The ticket holds the table's order information in precise shorthand. The chef expedites and coordinates the orders of as many as 20 tables at once. When the kitchen staff received the ticket for table 7 from Bonnie, the cooks on the first course station produced the appetizers and the meat station staff began organizing their part in the coming entrées. At the fire call, the vegetable cook joins the action, preparing a variety of accompaniments for each main course. The fish cooks begin their part in the production. Within minutes, all stations have completed their contributions and the chef and sous-chef are making last-second adjustments at the finishing station. The chef gives Bonnie final instructions as she leaves to deliver the plates to the guests' table. Team Cuisine is in action.

First courses are like the opening notes of a symphony, the prelude to the main act. At the Inn, they set the stage for the show to come and spark the appetite. In the guise of a few mouthfuls, first courses serve to present the chef's credentials for evaluation by the guests.

First courses are an opportunity to show off a particularly compelling ingredient or presentation. Guests seem to be more adventurous in ordering new or unfamiliar things for the beginning of their meal. Very often in my preparations I use ingredients that are so flavorful or rich that only a small portion is appropriate. Six ounces of smoked salmon served as a main course would be a bit overwhelming for most of our guests. A first course can also be a place to use a particularly expensive ingredient in moderation, making it more affordable.

The world's tallest house salad!

Every year thousands of oysters are served at the Inn.

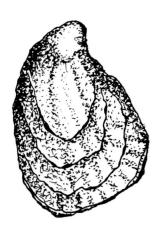

A Malpeque Oyster Tasting: Some Hot, Some Cold, All Different

The Malpeque oysters of Prince Edward Island are world famous for their pristine flavor and natural brininess. If Malpeque oysters are unavailable in your area, use another variety, preferably local. We serve our guests a sampler of six oysters, each prepared in a way that does not mask the oyster's flavor.

6 OYSTERS PER SERVING

(See the color photo illustrating the presentation of the oysters.)

Potato Crusted Oysters

Crisp and crunchy — these oysters are a delight.

6 large oysters	½ cup all-purpose flour
1 egg	½ cup instant mashed potato flakes
1 tablespoon water	4 tablespoons butter

CAREFULLY shuck the oysters, remove the meat, and discard the upper shells. Reserve the lower shells with their cup-shaped indentations. Pat the oysters dry on paper towels.

BEAT together the egg and the water. Dredge the oysters first in the flour, then in the egg mixture, and finally in the potato flakes.

IN a nonstick sauté pan, heat the butter until it is sizzling. Quickly add the oysters and brown them first on one side, then the other. Remove them from the pan, and place them on a paper towel for a moment. Transfer the oysters to their shells, and serve immediately.

Oysters with Vermouth Sabayon

Sabayon is a foamy and intensely flavored sauce. It highlights the wine used to make it, and in this recipe complements the oysters perfectly.

6 large oysters	Black pepper
2 egg yolks	Salt
4 tablespoons white dry vermouth	

CHEF'S HINTS

If you don't have an oyster knife, a can opener or a heavy screwdriver can be used to open an oyster. Protect the hand holding the oyster with a heavy glove in case the tool slips. ✳ It is important to fry the oysters quickly: the frying should just crisp the coating while only warming the oyster within. In our kitchen, it takes no more than 30 or 40 seconds to execute this method. ✳ Use a sauté pan that is big enough so that the oysters are not crowded, but not so big that they are lost.

CAREFULLY shuck the oysters. Discard the upper shells, and leave the meat nestled in the cup-shaped portion of the lower shells.

IN a stainless steel bowl, whisk together the egg yolks, vermouth, a little pepper, and a pinch of salt. Place the bowl over a medium-sized pot of simmering water. Whisk the egg mixture vigorously for several minutes until it doubles in volume and begins to thicken. When it is thick enough to hold its shape, remove it from the heat. The sabayon will be hot to the touch. Place a dollop of sabayon on each oyster and serve immediately.

OYSTERS WITH JUNIPER PICKLED RED ONIONS

The sweet acidity of these pickled onions goes well with the brininess of the oysters. Prepare the pickled onions the day before you plan to serve them. Their flavor is remarkably enhanced by the aromatic juniper — an evergreen berry used to flavor gin — available from your local specialty food store. Any extra onions can be used as a condiment with meat or fish.

3 tablespoons whole juniper berries
1 cup sugar
1 cup red wine vinegar

1 teaspoon Tabasco
1 large red onion, sliced into thin rings
6 large oysters

USE a small electric coffee grinder to grind the juniper berries. You may also place them in a clean towel and crush them with a hammer. Combine the berries with the sugar and vinegar in a small saucepan. Bring the berry mixture to a simmer, and cook it gently for 5 minutes. Turn off the heat, add the Tabasco, and let the syrup stand for 30 minutes. Strain it to remove any juniper pieces and bring it to a simmer once more.

PLACE the onion rings in a container and pour the syrup over them. Cover the onion mixture and refrigerate it for at least 12 hours.

CAREFULLY shuck the oysters. Discard the upper shells, and leave the meat nestled in the cup-shaped portion of the lower shells. Place a spoonful of the pickled onions on each oyster, and serve immediately.

CHEF'S HINTS

Sabayon is very fragile. It will flatten after a few minutes when left to stand. ✷ Don't allow the bottom of the bowl to touch the water in the pot — the bowl should be suspended over the water. The space between them insulates the egg from the heat. If the pot is too small, the heat may travel up the outside of the pot to the bowl and scorch the egg.

CHEF'S HINTS

Electric coffee grinders are very useful for grinding spices. ✷ When storing the pickled onions, make sure that the syrup completely covers them so that they will pickle evenly.

CHEF'S HINTS

The zest is the key to the flavor of the citrus ice. ✳ By heating the juice, you allow the sugar to melt and the full flavor of the oil in the zest to permeate the syrup. ✳ The syrup should be about 1 inch deep in the pan in which it is frozen. This thickness will make it easy to scrape the ice.

OYSTERS WITH SPICY CITRUS ICE

Frozen citrus juice is a refreshing, tangy accompaniment for oysters.

3 limes	1 teaspoon Tabasco
2 lemons	¼ teaspoon salt
2 oranges	6 large oysters
3 tablespoons sugar	

USING a citrus zester, zest the fruit. Mince the zest. Squeeze the fruit and place the juice in a small saucepan. Add the zest, sugar, Tabasco, and salt. Bring the mixture to a simmer, and then remove it from the heat. Pour the citrus syrup into a shallow pan. Wrap the pan tightly with plastic wrap, and place in the freezer until the syrup freezes.

CAREFULLY shuck the oysters. Discard the upper shells, and leave the meat nestled in the cup-shaped portion of the lower shells.

USING a spoon, scrape the ice into shards and place a spoonful on each oyster. Serve immediately.

OYSTERS WITH SMOKED SALMON AND DIJON MUSTARD

The flavors of smoke and brine are what make these oysters so delicious.

6 large oysters	1 tablespoon extra virgin olive oil
6 slices smoked salmon, about 1 by 3 inches	1 tablespoon sour cream
2 tablespoons Dijon mustard	

CAREFULLY shuck the oysters, remove the meat, and discard the upper shells. Reserve the lower shells with their cup-shaped indentations.

ROLL each oyster in a salmon slice. Place the wrapped oysters in the reserved shells, tucking the ends of the salmon slices under the oysters.

CHEF'S HINTS

Use a high-quality smoked salmon for this recipe. If you're a true connoisseur, slice some very fresh raw salmon and use it in place of the smoked salmon. ✳ For a more attractive presentation, use a small squeeze bottle, such as a ketchup container, to squeeze the Dijon mustard mixture onto the oysters.

WHISK together the mustard, oil, and sour cream. Place a dollop of the mixture on each oyster. Serve immediately.

OYSTERS WITH CHIVE SOUR CREAM AND ALLSPICE PEPPER

The oyster flavor shines in this simple, classic recipe.

6 large oysters
2 tablespoons sour cream
2 teaspoons chive oil (page 68)

Salt
Allspice pepper (page 66)

CAREFULLY shuck the oysters. Discard the upper shells, and leave the meat nestled in the cup-shaped portion of the lower shells.

WHISK together the sour cream, chive oil, and a pinch of salt. Place a dollop of the sour cream mixture on each oyster. Grind a little of the allspice pepper onto each oyster, and serve immediately.

WINE: Light- to medium-bodied dry white wine such as a California Sauvignon Blanc or Chablis.

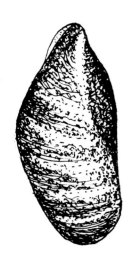

ISLAND BLUE MUSSEL AND SWEET POTATO CHOWDER WITH SPICY BUTTER SWIRLS

This is the single most requested recipe at the Inn, and a great way to show off the sweetness of our native mussels. Prince Edward Island mussels are available all over North America. They are easy to work with, their beards have been removed for you, and they are grit free because they are farm raised.

4 TO 6 SERVINGS

ISLAND BLUE MUSSEL AND SWEET POTATO CHOWDER

5 pounds island blue mussels

4 tablespoons water

1 large onion, chopped (about 2 cups)

4 tablespoons butter

4 cloves garlic, chopped

2 medium carrots, grated

2 medium sweet potatoes, grated

2 cups milk

1 cup heavy cream

1 teaspoon Bay Fortune seasoning (page 66)

1 teaspoon salt

1 teaspoon Tabasco

PLACE the mussels and water in a pot with a tight fitting lid. Place the pot over high heat and steam the mussels for 10 to 12 minutes until the shells open. Discard any mussels that don't open. Remove the meat from the shells and set the meat aside, and reserve some shells to use in the presentation. Strain and reserve the remaining liquid.

IN a large pot, sauté the onion in the butter over high heat for about 10 minutes. Stir frequently, and turn the heat down slightly every few minutes to prevent burning. Add the garlic and continue cooking until the onion is golden brown. Add the carrot, sweet potato, milk, cream, Bay Fortune seasoning, salt, Tabasco, and 1 cup of the mussel broth. Bring the mixture to a boil, reduce the heat to low, cover the pot, and let it simmer gently for 30 minutes. Stir frequently to prevent scorching on the bottom of the pot. (While it is simmering, make the spicy butter.) After 30 minutes, check the vegetables for doneness. If they are soft, remove the pot from the heat. If they are still slightly al dente, simmer a few minutes longer or until done.

PURÉE the soup thoroughly in a blender, and strain through a fine mesh strainer. If necessary, adjust the consistency of the soup with the remaining mussel liquid. The soup should be pleasantly thick but not goopy.

CHEF'S HINTS

It is important not to overcook the mussels. Steam them for only a few minutes after the shells have opened; the mussels should stay plump and juicy. ✳ Let the reserved mussel liquid stand, and some sediment may settle to the bottom of the pot. Carefully pour out the liquid, avoiding the harmless silt. ✳ Using a blender is the best way to get a perfectly smooth soup, but a food processor will work almost as well.

RETURN the soup to the pot and heat it, stirring frequently, until it is almost at serving temperature. Add the reserved mussel meat, and heat, stirring, for a few minutes until heated through. Serve the chowder immediately with the spicy butter.

SPICY BUTTER SWIRLS

2 tablespoons butter

2 tablespoons heavy cream

2 tablespoons molasses

½ tablespoon Tabasco

¼ teaspoon ground allspice

¼ teaspoon ground cloves

PUT the butter, cream, molasses, Tabasco, allspice, and cloves in a small saucepan and bring the mixture to a simmer, stirring frequently. Remove from the heat, and allow the mixture to cool to room temperature.

PRESENTATION

Mussel shells

LADLE the soup into warmed bowls. Drizzle the spicy butter around the surface of the soup. Gently shake each bowl to swirl the butter slightly. You may also pull a toothpick through the butter to create patterns. Use a few of the mussel shells to garnish the soup, or tuck them in between the bowl and its underliner.

WINE: Light- to medium-bodied off-dry to lightly sweet white wine such as Chenin Blanc or Vouvray.

Caramel and Horseradish Apple Soups with Sharp Cheddar Fritters and Spicy Apple Chutney

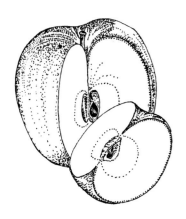

In this recipe for special occasions, two soups are combined to form a balanced combination of tastes. The flavors are old friends, and the fritters and chutney complete the presentation.

6 SERVINGS

TIMING: Make the chutney and refrigerate overnight. ✴ Make the fritter batter and refrigerate for 60 minutes. ✴ Remove the chutney from the refrigerator to warm. ✴ Make the soups. ✴ Cook the fritters and warm the soups.

Spicy Apple Chutney

1 cup sugar
½ cup water
2 large onions, chopped (about 4 cups)
2 Granny Smith apples, peeled, cored, and
    finely chopped (about 3 cups)

½ cup cider vinegar
1 teaspoon Bay Fortune seasoning (page 66)
1 teaspoon ground allspice
1 teaspoon Tabasco
½ teaspoon salt

FOLLOWING the instructions on page 67, form a caramel with the sugar and water, then shock the caramel with the onion. Stir and cook the onion in the caramel until most of the liquid has evaporated.

ADD the apple, vinegar, Bay Fortune seasoning, allspice, Tabasco, and salt, and bring to a simmer. Cook for 5 minutes over medium heat, stirring gently. Remove the chutney from the heat, place in a storage container, and refrigerate overnight. Remove the chutney from the refrigerator in time to reach room temperature before serving.

Sharp Cheddar Fritters

¼ cup all-purpose flour
½ teaspoon salt
¼ teaspoon baking powder
¼ cup milk

2 tablespoons butter
1 cup grated sharp cheddar cheese
1 egg, beaten
4 cups vegetable oil

SIFT together the flour, salt, and baking powder in a bowl. In a medium-sized saucepan, bring the milk and butter to a simmer. Add the flour mixture to the milk mixture all at once, and stir vigorously until a smooth paste is formed.

PLACE the flour paste in a food processor. Add the cheese and egg, and process until thoroughly incorporated and the mixture forms a smooth paste again. Remove the batter, place it in a storage container, and refrigerate for 60 minutes or so. (Meanwhile, prepare the soups.)

PREHEAT the oven to 300°F.

IN a high-sided pan, heat the oil until it reaches 350°F. Using 2 teaspoons, form the batter into evenly shaped fritters (12 in total) no more than 1 inch thick, and drop them carefully into the hot oil. Don't fill the pan. Fry just a few fritters at a time, turning them frequently so they brown on all sides. When the fritters have plumped up and are golden brown, remove them with a slotted spoon and drain them on paper towels. Heat the oil again, and continue forming and frying fritters until the batter is all used. Reheat the fritters in the oven for a few minutes, and serve immediately.

CARAMEL APPLE SOUP

½ cup sugar
¼ cup water
1 large onion, chopped (about 2 cups)
2 Granny Smith apples, peeled, cored, and
  chopped (about 3 cups)

3 cups cider
2 teaspoons salt
½ tablespoon ground cinnamon

FOLLOWING the instructions on page 67, form a caramel with the sugar and water, then shock the caramel with the onion.

STIR and cook the onion in the caramel until the latter is completely dissolved. Continue cooking until the moisture in the onion evaporates and the onion begins to brown. When the onion has caramelized, add the apple, cider, salt, and cinnamon, and bring the mixture to a boil. Cover the pot, reduce the heat to a simmer, and cook for 20 minutes.

CHEF'S HINTS

The batter is easier to work with when it has been left to stand for an hour. ✳ Before you begin frying, practice forming the fritters until they are a consistent shape. The fritters should be tapered and have pointed ends, and vaguely resemble a football. Any shape will work; the trick is to be consistent.

CHEF'S HINTS

This soup will benefit from being stored overnight in the refrigerator; the flavors will combine and become more pronounced. Reheat it slowly in a saucepan, stirring frequently. ✳ A food processor can also be used to purée the soup, but it won't be as smooth.

POUR the soup into a blender, and purée thoroughly. Strain through a fine mesh strainer, and set aside.

WARM the soup, stirring frequently, while the fritters are being cooked. The soup may also be made ahead and refrigerated.

HORSERADISH APPLE SOUP

1 large onion, chopped (about 2 cups)

1 tablespoon butter

2 Granny Smith apples, peeled, cored, and chopped (about 3 cups)

2 cups apple juice

1 cup Chardonnay

½ cup prepared horseradish

2 teaspoons salt

1 teaspoon ground nutmeg

IN a large pot, sauté the onion in the butter until the onion is translucent. Add the apple, apple juice, wine, horseradish, salt, and nutmeg, and bring to a boil. Reduce the heat until the soup is just simmering, then cover the pot with a tight fitting lid. Cook for 20 minutes, or until the apples are very soft.

POUR the soup into a blender and purée thoroughly. Strain through a fine mesh strainer, and set aside.

WARM the soup, stirring frequently, while the fritters are being cooked. The soup may also be made ahead and refrigerated.

PRESENTATION

USE 6 warm, broad, shallow soup bowls. Rest the bottom of each soup bowl on the edge of an overturned plate so that the bowl is slightly tilted. Ladle one of the soups into the lower part of the bowl. As you tilt the bowl back to level with your other hand, ladle the second soup into the other side of the bowl. Place a scoop of chutney in the center of each bowl, top with 2 fritters, and serve.

WINE: Spicy, light- to medium-bodied off-dry to lightly sweet white wine such as Riesling.

Strawberry Gazpacho with Strawberry Salsa, Black Pepper Croutons, and Balsamic Vinegar Strawberry Purée

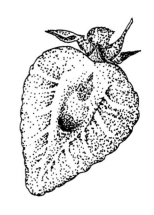

Often at home in savory preparations as well as desserts, strawberries have a natural affinity for balsamic vinegar. This unique soup unites the flavor of the strawberries and the vinegar with other classically inspired gazpacho elements.

4 SERVINGS

Timing: Make the gazpacho and the salsa and refrigerate overnight. ✳ Make the croutons. ✳ Make the purée.

Strawberry Gazpacho

1 pound strawberries, puréed (about 4 cups)
½ cup extra virgin olive oil
¼ cup balsamic vinegar
½ teaspoon salt

Place the strawberries, oil, vinegar, and salt in a blender, and process thoroughly until the mixture is smooth and glossy. Do not strain. Place in a container and refrigerate overnight. Stir the gazpacho well before serving.

Strawberry Salsa

½ cup diced strawberries
¼ cup finely diced green pepper
¼ cup finely diced red onion
2 tablespoons thinly sliced mint
½ tablespoon balsamic vinegar
½ tablespoon extra virgin olive oil
1 teaspoon minced jalapeño
¼ teaspoon salt

Place the strawberries, green pepper, onion, mint, vinegar, oil, jalapeño, and salt in a bowl. Toss the mixture gently to combine the ingredients without bruising the berries. Refrigerate the salsa overnight.

CHEF'S HINTS

Don't use the unripe fresh strawberries available in many supermarkets. This recipe is best made with local, freshly picked berries that are juicy and flavorful. ✳ Use the most flavorful olive oil available.

CHEF'S HINT

Fresh spearmint, which has a particularly clean and sharp flavor, is the best mint for this salsa.

Black Pepper Croutons

2 slices black pepper yeast bread (page 48), cut into ½-inch cubes (about 2 cups)

2 tablespoons extra virgin olive oil

PREHEAT the oven to 400°F.

TOSS the bread cubes in the oil. Place them on a baking sheet, and bake until they are toasted and golden brown, about 10 minutes.

Balsamic Vinegar Strawberry Purée

¼ cup balsamic vinegar
¼ cup diced strawberries

½ tablespoon extra virgin olive oil

IN a small saucepan, bring the vinegar to a simmer and reduce it by half. Purée the reduced vinegar with the berries and oil in a blender. Pour the purée into a squeeze bottle, and reserve until the soup is served.

Presentation

Mint sprigs

POUR the chilled soup into chilled broad, shallow soup bowls. Squeeze the strawberry purée in a decorative pattern onto the surface of the soup. Add a spoonful of the salsa. Form a pile of the toasted croutons in the center of the bowl, top with a mint sprig, and serve immediately.

WINE: Spicy, light- to medium-bodied off-dry to lightly sweet white wine such as Gewürztraminer.

CHEF'S HINT

Reducing the vinegar intensifies its flavor but weakens its acidity. A combination of reduced and unreduced vinegar will make the purée more flavorful when a mild tasting balsamic vinegar is used.

Smoked Salmon Rye Bread Pudding with Dill Yogurt Sauce, Dijon Mousse, and Juniper Pickled Red Onions

This recipe combines classic flavors in a new way, and makes a tasty brunch dish. I enjoy using smoked salmon as an element of a recipe in which it is combined with other flavors. Juniper pickled red onions (page 79) and dill sprigs complete the presentation.

6 SERVINGS

TIMING: Make the pickled onions and refrigerate for at least 12 hours. ✳ Remove the pickled onions from the refrigerator to warm. ✳ Make the bread pudding. ✳ Make the sauce and the mousse.

Smoked Salmon Rye Bread Pudding

4 to 5 slices dark rye bread, cut into
 ½-inch cubes (about 5 cups)
3 whole eggs
2 egg yolks
1 tablespoon Dijon mustard
2 cups milk

1 teaspoon salt
½ teaspoon black pepper
½ teaspoon ground caraway seeds
8 ounces unsliced smoked salmon, cut into
 ½-inch cubes (about 1 cup)

CHEF'S HINTS

Toasting the rye bread both dries it out so that it absorbs more liquid and intensifies its flavor. ✳ Letting the pudding mixture stand for 30 minutes allows the bread to absorb the liquid. ✳ A wide variety of baking containers may be used. A large muffin pan will work, or you can bake the pudding in one container. ✳ The cooking time is dependent on the size of the baking vessel.

PREHEAT the oven to 350°F. Butter 6 (8-ounce) ramekins, soufflé dishes, or other small baking dishes.

TOAST the bread cubes until crisp, about 10 to 15 minutes. Remove them from the oven and reserve.

IN a large mixing bowl, whisk together the whole egg, egg yolk, and mustard. Add the milk, salt, pepper, and caraway, and combine. Add the bread cubes and salmon, and toss gently to combine thoroughly. Cover the bowl, and refrigerate the pudding mixture for 30 minutes.

BRING a kettle of water to the boil.

TOSS the ingredients gently once more and divide evenly between the ramekins.

PLACE a baking or roasting pan large enough to hold all the ramekins in the oven. Fill the pan with enough hot water to come halfway up their sides. Place the ramekins in the water and add more hot water until it is almost all the way to the top of the ramekins.

BAKE until the edges of the puddings begin to puff and the center sets, about 35 to 45 minutes. Remove the puddings from the oven and let them cool for 10 minutes before serving.

DILL YOGURT SAUCE

Juice and zest of 1 lemon   ½ cup dill sprigs
1 cup yogurt   Salt

MINCE the lemon zest. In a blender, process the lemon juice and zest, yogurt, dill, and a pinch of salt until smooth. Place the sauce in a squeeze bottle and reserve.

DIJON MOUSSE

1 cup whipping cream   Black pepper
½ cup Dijon mustard   Salt

IN a large bowl, stir together the cream, mustard, some freshly ground pepper, and a pinch of salt. Whip the cream mixture until stiff.

PRESENTATION

(See the color photo illustrating the presentation of this dish.)

Juniper pickled red onions   Dill sprigs

USING the squeeze bottle, decorate 6 plates with streaks of yogurt sauce. Run a thin-bladed knife blade around the edge of each pudding to loosen it from the sides of the ramekin. Invert the puddings onto the plates. Place a spoonful of juniper pickled red onions and a dollop of the Dijon mousse on each pudding. Crown with a dill sprig and serve immediately.

WINE: Light- to medium-bodied dry white wine such as Aligote or Chablis.

POTATO, BACON, AND CHEDDAR TART WITH HORSERADISH BROTH AND SPINACH

Making this potato tart is a detailed process, but the results are spectacular.

6 TO 8 SERVINGS

POTATO, BACON, AND CHEDDAR TART

1½ pounds bacon slices, at room temperature
Black pepper
3 cups grated sharp cheddar cheese
5 to 7 large baking potatoes (about 2½ to
  3½ pounds)

Salt
1 cup minced onion
1 head garlic, peeled and minced

PREHEAT the oven to 325°F.

LINE a 9-inch cast-iron skillet with parchment paper. Spray it lightly with vegetable oil. Trim the edges of the paper so it just clears the top edge of the pan. Carefully arrange the bacon slices in a radial pattern from the center of the pan to the lower edge, then up and over the rim. Let the ends hang over the rim. The slices should overlap slightly around the sides of the pan; the bacon will be thicker in the pan's center. To reduce the thickness of the bacon in the center, stagger every other piece of bacon, starting it 2 inches from the center and extending it farther than the adjacent slices (see drawing). With the palm of your hand, flatten the center area, leaving no holes through the bacon. Grind some pepper onto the bacon, and sprinkle on 2 tablespoons of the grated cheddar.

WITHOUT peeling them, slice the potatoes thinly. The slices should be uniform, and about ¼ inch thick. Arrange a circular layer of overlapping potato slices on top of the bacon around the edge of the skillet. Continue arranging rings of overlapping potato until the bottom of the pan is evenly covered. Sprinkle the potato with salt and freshly ground pepper.

IN a bowl, mix together the onion and garlic. Sprinkle some of the onion mixture onto the first potato layer, then follow with a layer of the cheese. Cover with another layer of potato, pressing it down firmly before adding more seasoning. Repeat these layering steps until the potato reaches the top of the skillet. Add 2 more layers rising above the top of the pan, ending with a layer of potato. The final layers should each be inset 1 inch from the previous layer.

TAKING 1 slice at a time, fold the bacon up and over the potato mound toward the center. Carefully overlap each slice, and repeat until the top is completely and neatly covered with bacon. Trim a small piece of parchment paper, and place it in between a small ovenproof lid

CHEF'S HINTS

If you can't find parchment paper, ask your favorite baker or restaurant waiter if you can have a sheet. ✳ Use the best, leanest, bacon you can find — cheap bacon will shrink and tear. Let the bacon warm to room temperature before using it, so it will stretch slightly and be easier to work with. ✳ Use baking potatoes: their high starch content will help them adhere to each other as they bake. Other types will cause the tart to collapse.

and the bacon. The lid is only meant to weigh the bacon ends down during the baking so they don't pull away and shrink. Don't use a large lid that will slow down the tart's baking time. Leave the lid on while the tart bakes.

PLACE the tart on a baking sheet, and put it in the oven. Bake it about 3 to 3½ hours. (While it is baking, make the broth.) It is done when a thin-bladed knife inserted into it meets no resistance. The bacon will have browned and tightened, forming a crust, and the potatoes will have shrunk. Pour off any excess fat that is inside the pan. Let the tart stand for 30 minutes so that it will solidify.

HORSERADISH BROTH

½ cup water
6 slices bacon, chopped
1½ cups minced onion
6 cloves garlic, minced
¾ cup Cabernet Sauvignon

2 cups roast chicken broth (page 69)
½ cup prepared horseradish
1 teaspoon minced rosemary
Salt

PLACE the water and bacon in a small saucepan. Over medium heat, bring the bacon mixture to a simmer and evaporate the water, stirring frequently. Continue cooking until the bacon is crisp. Add the onion and continue cooking until it begins to brown. Add the garlic and stir for a few minutes longer.

ADD the wine and stir until all the browned bits on the bottom of the pot are loosened. Add the chicken broth, horseradish, and rosemary. Bring the broth to a simmer, reduce the heat, and simmer for 20 minutes. Check the broth before serving and add a pinch of salt if needed.

PRESENTATION

Spinach leaves

INVERT the tart onto a plate, and peel off the parchment paper. Cut into wedges. Place a handful of spinach leaves in warm, wide, shallow soup bowls. Pour ¼ cup of the hot broth over the spinach in each bowl. Place a wedge of the tart on top of the spinach, and serve immediately.

WINE: Light- to medium-bodied dry red wine such as Côtes du Rhône.

CHEF'S HINTS

By using the water when cooking the bacon, you speed up the rendering process without the risk of burning the bacon. ✴ If you don't have homemade chicken broth, use a high-quality, low-sodium canned variety.

8:30 pm: Bonnie graciously presents the main courses to the guests at table 7. As she enters the service station, Bonnie updates her serving partner on the status of the tables: "I've just sat tables 1 and 3, 6 and 11 have menus and muses, I need two glasses of Pinot Noir for the couple from Texas in the living room, and table 4 would like to see the kitchen and meet the chef!" Bonnie's partner then updates Bonnie on the status of the other tables. As a lead server, Bonnie must know the exact progress of every guest in the dining room. Another server arrives to hurry them away for a coordinated swoop of a large table. They clear it and head for the kitchen. Bonnie shows the empty plates to the chef as she delivers them to the dishwasher. Spinning, she encounters him again. He hands her two more plates: "Table 8 please." Smiling, she heads for the dining room.

M ain courses are the stars of a menu, the marquee names that make a restaurant famous. They are the culmination of a chef's ability to combine ideas, flavors, and textures in a distinctive way. Main courses show off the varied talents of the restaurant's kitchen staff, the polished precision of a team of focused cooks.

The unique main courses served at The Inn at Bay Fortune are carefully constructed culinary statements. They are

"Off to table 8."

a combination of harmonious ingredients, each contributing to the overall flavor of the dish. The components are prepared in a manner that maximizes their role. The sauces are made with a specific presentation in mind. There are no ubiquitous parsley sprigs. Each and every detail is relevant.

Entrée courses are subject to more scrutiny than other menu elements. These courses represent the core of the meal and can define the dining experience. At the Inn, we commonly pair a main protein with a sauce, starch, and vegetables, but doing so is a nod to tradition, not a restrictive formula. Our self-imposed challenge is to make every element on a plate complement its neighbors. No ingredient is used arbitrarily.

The following menu items and their corresponding recipes represent a moment in time, but the techniques presented are flexible and easily altered by interpretation. On any given day at the Inn, the ingredients available and the whim of the chef influence the specific combinations represented here. If you duplicate these recipes, the results will be wonderful; if you adapt the methods and modify them with your own influences, they become yours.

Jennifer, a cook, and the sous-chef discuss a recipe detail.

9:57 pm: The action is starting to die down. Most tables have already been served, and only a few tickets remain hanging from the expeditor's board. The height of the rush has passed, and there's an air of accomplishment in the kitchen. The chef is preparing to tour the dining room when the vegetable cook announces with dread, "We're out of chanterelles. I need four orders to cover the board." Sold out! Without hesitation, the chef says, "Get a flashlight. Let's get some more." He and the cook bolt for the back door, headed for the mushroom patch in the woods behind the Inn. "Put a pan on the flame, we'll be right back," shouts the chef as the door slams. In minutes they return, and the lamb with chanterelles is soon on its way to the guests' table.

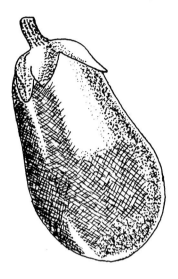

Spice Rubbed Tuna Loin with Saffron Ratatouille, Tomato Anchovy Sauce, and Swiss Chard

The classic flavors of the Mediterranean are part of every chef's repertoire. This recipe shows how we combine them with locally caught tuna.

Saffron is a perfect addition to the rich flavors of ratatouille, which is essentially a vegetable stew. When made carefully, this ratatouille has a wonderful flavor. Prepare the ratatouille the day before you plan to serve it — it will taste even better as its flavors blossom.

Have four large Swiss chard leaves ready for the presentation.

4 SERVINGS

TIMING: Make the ratatouille and refrigerate overnight. ✴ Make the anchovy sauce. ✴ Bring a pot of salted water to the boil for scalding the chard. ✴ Cook the tuna as you begin the presentation steps.

CHEF'S HINTS

The aim of this method is to create a cohesive mixture that retains the essence of each of its elements. By not cooking all the vegetables together, this ratatouille avoids becoming a dull looking, plain tasting stew. ✴ Don't use pale, lifeless supermarket tomatoes: if you can't find fresh, vine-ripened tomatoes, use canned tomatoes.

Saffron Ratatouille

1 cup minced onion	½ teaspoon saffron threads
3 tablespoons extra virgin olive oil	1 cup chopped eggplant
4 cloves garlic, minced	1 cup chopped green pepper
1 cup chopped tomato	1 cup chopped zucchini
1 teaspoon minced jalapeño	1 teaspoon salt

IN a saucepan, cook the onion in 1 tablespoon of the oil until golden brown. Add the garlic and continue cooking for several minutes more. Add the tomato, jalapeño, and saffron. Turn the heat to low, and continue cooking until much of the liquid has evaporated, about 15 minutes.

WHILE the tomato mixture is simmering, heat 1 tablespoon of the remaining oil in a nonstick sauté pan over high heat. Add the eggplant, and sauté until it is just cooked through. Place the eggplant in a large bowl, and set aside. Sauté the green pepper in ½ tablespoon of the remaining oil until brightly colored and just cooked through. Place the green pepper in the bowl with the eggplant. Follow the same procedure to cook the zucchini to the same degree of doneness, and add the zucchini to the eggplant and green pepper.

POUR the tomato mixture over the eggplant, green pepper, and zucchini. Add the salt, and toss the mixture until completely mixed. Refrigerate overnight.

THE EVOLUTION OF A PLATE IN THE OPEN KITCHEN
SPICE RUBBED TUNA LOIN WITH SAFFRON RATATOUILLE, TOMATO ANCHOVY SAUCE, AND SWISS CHARD, PAGE 96

1. Simple tools can be used to create a unique presentation. Start with a ring mold on a large plate.

2. Line the mold with the just-blanched Swiss chard leaf, pressing it gently into place.

3. Fill the leaf with the hot ratatouille.

4. Fold over the ends of the leaf.

5. Invert a small plate onto the mold, flip both plates over, remove the large plate, and use a spatula to transfer the mold and its contents back to the large plate.

6. Carefully remove the mold by lifting it straight up.

7. Ladle the hot sauce onto the plate and arrange the tuna slices.

8. Add some baby vegetables.

9. The finishing touches, et voilà.

Spice Rubbed Tuna Loin
with Saffron Ratatouille,
Tomato Anchovy Sauce,
and Swiss Chard
(page 96)

A Time for Chocolate:
Molten Bittersweet Chocolate Cake
with Cookie Clock Hands,
Allspice Pepper Sautéed Bananas, and Rum Froth
(page 135)

Roasted Carrot Cake with Cream Cheese Sauce, Carrot Ice, and Minted Carrots in Riesling Syrup (page 138)

Tomato Anchovy Sauce

Juice and zest of 1 lemon

2 medium tomatoes, puréed (about 1 cup)

6 anchovies, oil or brine squeezed out*

4 tablespoons extra virgin olive oil

½ teaspoon Tabasco

Use salt cured anchovies if available. They are of higher quality.

RESERVE 1 tablespoon of the lemon juice for another use. Combine the remaining lemon juice, lemon zest, tomato, anchovies, oil, and Tabasco in a blender, and process until very smooth.

STRAIN the sauce through a fine mesh strainer. Set aside.

Spice Rubbed Tuna Loin

1 tablespoon Bay Fortune seasoning
 (page 66)

1 tablespoon coarsely ground black pepper

1 tablespoon Hungarian paprika*

4 tuna steaks (6 ounces each, about 1½ inches thick), chilled

4 tablespoons extra virgin olive oil

Paprika making has a long tradition in Hungary, which produces the best paprika. Look for it in your local supermarket or specialty food store.

COMBINE the Bay Fortune seasoning, pepper, and paprika in a small bowl. Pat the fish dry, then thoroughly and evenly coat the tuna steaks with the spice mixture, pressing it into the fish.

PREHEAT a large cast-iron skillet over high heat for several minutes. Add the oil and heat it until it is very hot. When wisps of smoke just begin to show, quickly add the tuna steaks. Sear on one side for 2 to 3 minutes until crisp, then turn the steaks over and sear the other side. (Begin the presentation steps as you are cooking the tuna.) Serve immediately.

CHEF'S HINTS

To preserve the freshness of the flavors in the sauce, it is heated just before serving.
✳ Depending on the brininess of the anchovies, it may be necessary to add a pinch of salt to balance the sauce.

CHEF'S HINTS

Ask your trusty fishmonger for yellowfin or bigeye tuna. It must be absolutely fresh.
✳ Tuna is best served with the center still raw and cool. A thick steak will allow you to sear the outside without the heat penetrating to the center. Chilling the fish will also retard heat penetration. A cast-iron skillet works well because it absorbs and releases heat evenly. Make sure the pan is very hot before adding the fish, or the fish will overcook as the pan heats to searing temperature.

PRESENTATION

(See the color photos illustrating the presentation of this dish.)

4 large Swiss chard leaves

REHEAT the ratatouille in a microwave, or in a saucepan on medium heat. Reheat the tomato anchovy sauce. Meanwhile, bring a pot of salted water to the boil. Dip each chard leaf into the boiling water briefly, just long enough to wilt the leaf.

FIT the leaf into a 4-inch wide circular mold about 1-inch tall. (At the Inn we use PVC pipe cut to our specifications.) Fill the leaf-lined mold with ratatouille. Fold the ends of the leaf over at the top to seal it. Invert the filled mold onto a warm dinner plate. Carefully remove the mold by gently lifting it directly up. Repeat for each plate.

POUR the sauce onto the plate in 3 places, framing the ratatouille. Cut each tuna steak into 3 pieces, and arrange them around the plate. Serve immediately.

WINE: Full-bodied dry white wine such as Chardonnay or Macon-Villages, or medium-bodied Pinot Noir.

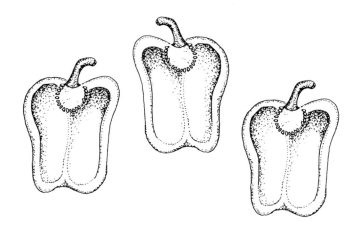

Blue Cheese Crusted Beef Tenderloin with Brown Butter Potatoes, Asparagus, and Cabernet Sauvignon Sauce

This recipe is a combination of comfortable, familiar flavors. At the Inn, we tend not to be too elaborate with beef dishes. The method used in the sauce accentuates the flavor of the Cabernet Sauvignon. The richly flavored potatoes are a perfect complement.

4 SERVINGS

TIMING: Make the sauce and keep warm. ✳ Make the potato and keep warm. ✳ Bake the steak. ✳ Cook the asparagus.

CABERNET SAUVIGNON SAUCE

2 cups Cabernet Sauvignon
2 cups heavy cream
1 cup minced shallots
2 cloves garlic, minced

½ teaspoon minced rosemary
½ teaspoon salt
¼ teaspoon black pepper

PLACE the wine, cream, shallots, garlic, rosemary, salt, and pepper in a saucepan, and bring to a boil. Reduce the heat, and simmer the sauce for 20 to 30 minutes until it has reduced in volume by half and the vegetables are tender.

POUR the sauce into a blender, and purée for several minutes until it is very smooth. Strain the sauce through a fine mesh strainer. Keep the sauce warm until needed.

BROWN BUTTER POTATOES

2 large potatoes, peeled (about 1½ pounds)
¼ pound butter (½ cup)
1 teaspoon salt

1 teaspoon white pepper
¼ teaspoon ground nutmeg

CUT each potato into 6 pieces (see drawing). Steam them until they are tender, about 15 minutes.

WHILE the potatoes are steaming, brown the butter following the instructions on page 67.

CHEF'S HINTS

The key to this sauce is the reduction of the wine and cream, which intensifies the flavor almost to the full flavor of the wine used. ✳ Virtually any wine will work with this method because the other ingredients do not overwhelm the flavor of the wine. ✳ The puréed, tender vegetables are the thickening agent for the sauce.

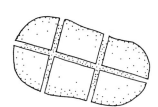

CHEF'S HINTS

Having the potato pieces a uniform size will help the heat penetrate the pieces without overcooking them.
✳ If you don't have a saucepan equipped with a steamer insert, use a steamer basket. Such baskets are inexpensive and invaluable. Boiling the potatoes will leach out some of their flavor.

PLACE the potato in a bowl and add the salt, pepper, and nutmeg. Using a mixer, whip the potato at medium speed, gradually adding the hot browned butter until it is thoroughly incorporated. Increase the mixer speed to high briefly to finish combining the potato and butter. Place the whipped potato in a covered dish, and keep it in the still warm oven until the steak and asparagus are ready.

VARIATIONS: For piquant mashed potato, whip in ¼ cup heavy cream, ¼ cup prepared horseradish, and a pinch of nutmeg. For green mashed potato, purée 1 cup chopped green onion stems with ¼ cup olive oil, and whip the onion mixture into the potato. For a brilliant purple and intensely flavored variation, reduce 1 cup Cabernet Sauvignon and 1 cup heavy cream to ½ cup, and whip into the potato.

BLUE CHEESE CRUSTED BEEF TENDERLOIN

¼ pound crumbled blue cheese
¼ pound plus 2 tablespoons butter
  (½ cup plus 2 tablespoons)
½ cup coarse dried bread crumbs

1 teaspoon minced rosemary
4 beef tenderloin steaks (about 6 ounces each),
  chilled
1 tablespoon coarsely ground black pepper

PREHEAT the oven to 400°F.

IN a food processor, process the blue cheese and the ¼ pound of butter into a smooth paste. Add the bread crumbs and rosemary, and continue processing until thoroughly combined. Set aside.

EVENLY coat each of the steaks with pepper, pressing it into the meat. Melt the remaining butter in a 10-inch nonstick skillet. When the butter begins to foam, place the steaks in the pan. Sear each side of the steaks, turning them once as they brown. (Refer to the section on roasting meat on page 70.) Watch carefully as you sear the meat and brown the butter. If the butter seems to be getting too hot, either turn the heat down slightly or baste the meat with several spoonfuls of the hot butter. When the steaks are evenly seared, place them on a cooling or roasting rack. Reserve the butter left in the pan for seasoning the asparagus.

PAT an even layer of the blue cheese paste onto the top of each steak. The paste should cover the entire top and extend slightly over the edges. Place the rack on a baking pan in the oven, and bake 10 to 15 minutes until the crust browns. Remove the steaks from the oven, and let them stand for 5 to 10 minutes before cutting them.

ASPARAGUS

12 spears asparagus, pencil thick   Black pepper
Reserved brown butter   Salt

TRIM the 1 inch or so at the bottom of each asparagus spear that is tough and woody. Thinly slice the asparagus into ¼-inch rounds, moving from the stem end toward the tip. Stop when 4 inches of the asparagus tip remain. Steam the asparagus until tender and still green, about 10 minutes. Toss the asparagus with a little of the reserved brown butter from the beef roasting, and season with pepper and salt.

PRESENTATION

4 rosemary sprigs

PLACE a neat pile of the brown butter potatoes in the center of a warm plate. Slice the beef diagonally from just under one edge of the crust down toward the bottom of the opposite side. Leave the crust intact. Arrange the 2 slices on the potatoes.

POUR ¼ cup of the sauce over the meat and onto the plate. Lean 3 asparagus spears between the slices of beef, and place a pile of the asparagus rounds at their bases. Garnish with a rosemary sprig, and serve immediately.

WINE: Full-bodied dry red wine such as Cabernet Sauvignon.

CHEF'S HINTS

You may use oil for the searing, but browning butter adds an extra dimension of flavor. Be patient when you first place the steaks in the pan or turn them over: constant handling will slow down the searing. ✳ The blue cheese paste may be made ahead of time.

North Side Scallops and South Side Clam Chowder with an In-Between Potato Crab Cake

Every seaside inn should have a signature chowder. This is ours. It's named after the source of the fish we use in our remote location. I don't often make such claims about the things that I cook, but this is the best chowder I've ever had.

The intense, celery-like flavor of the lovage is the key to this chowder. Although fresh lovage may be hard to find, its effect makes the search worthwhile. As with most chowders, the flavor of this one benefits greatly from being stored overnight.

6 SERVINGS

TIMING: Make the chowder and refrigerate overnight. ✳ Form the crab cakes and refrigerate for at least 60 minutes, or up to 1 day. ✳ Coat the crab cakes, which can be stored for several hours. ✳ Reheat the chowder and brown the crab cakes. ✳ Add the clams to the chowder and heat through, and pan sear the scallops.

SOUTH SIDE CLAM CHOWDER

CHEF'S HINTS

A variety of clams, including canned, work in this recipe. ✳ When steaming fresh clams, don't overcook them. When the shells open, the clams are almost done. Only another minute is needed to cook them through; any longer and they will become rubbery. ✳ Leaving the clam meat whole makes the chowder look more interesting when it is served. ✳ Be sure to taste the chowder before serving it, and add salt if necessary. The clams will add some salinity, but more may be needed. ✳ Cooling the chowder quickly will preserve the light green color that the herb purée gives.

5 pounds littleneck clams in the shell
¼ cup water
1 cup chopped onion
¼ pound butter (½ cup)
4 cloves garlic, minced
1 cup shredded potato

2 cups heavy cream
1 cup white dry vermouth
1 cup lovage leaves
1 teaspoon Tabasco
½ teaspoon salt

PLACE the clams in a large pot with a tight fitting lid. Add the water and steam the clams over medium heat until they open and heat through, about 10 minutes. Remove the meat from the shells, and reserve it in the refrigerator. Strain the remaining liquid through cheesecloth or a coffee filter. Reserve 1 cup of the clam liquid.

IN a thick-bottomed saucepan, sauté the onion in the butter until cooked through and translucent. Add the garlic and cook a few minutes longer. Add the potato, cream, wine, and reserved clam liquid. Bring the soup to a simmer, cover it, and cook for 20 minutes over low heat, stirring occasionally.

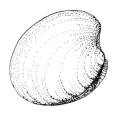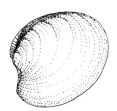

In batches, process the soup with the lovage in a blender until completely puréed. Add the Tabasco and the salt, and adjust the seasoning to taste.

Pour the chowder into a storage container and cool it rapidly by immersing it in an ice bath, stirring the chowder frequently as it cools. Refrigerate overnight.

Just before serving, gently reheat the chowder, stirring frequently. Add the clam meat and heat it through.

Potato Crab Cake

1 pound baking potatoes, peeled and diced (about 3 cups)
2 eggs, separated
1 pound fresh lump crab meat, well drained (about 2 cups)
½ cup snipped chives

1 teaspoon white pepper
1 teaspoon salt
1 tablespoon water
1 cup all-purpose flour
1 cup instant mashed potato flakes
4 tablespoons butter

Preheat the oven to 350°F. Lightly grease a baking sheet.

Steam the potato until tender. Pass it through a food mill, or mash it lightly with a fork. Spread the potato on the baking sheet and dry in the oven for 10 to 15 minutes, stirring occasionally. Let the potato cool for several minutes.

In a large bowl, whisk the egg white lightly until slightly frothy; reserve half of the egg white with the yolk in a separate bowl. To the egg white in the large bowl, add the mashed potato, crab, chives, pepper, and salt, and stir until completely combined. Form the mixture into 6 cylinder-shaped cakes, about 3 inches tall by 2 inches wide. Refrigerate for at least 60 minutes, or up to 1 day.

Whisk together the egg yolk and remaining egg white with the water. Roll the crab cakes in the flour, then dip them in the egg mixture, and finally roll them in the potato flakes. They may be stored in the refrigerator for several hours until you are ready to cook them.

Preheat the oven to 400°F. Heat the butter in a skillet over medium heat, and brown the crab cakes evenly, about 5 minutes. Place them in the oven and continue heating for 5 minutes.

CHEF'S HINTS

The moisture content of potatoes varies. Drying the potato is necessary to help the crab cakes bind. Feel the potato as it dries; it will feel dry to the touch when done. ✳ Try using a mold to form the crab cakes. They should be tall enough to protrude from the chowder when you serve it. ✳ As you are coating the crab cakes, take the time to shake off the excess flour and allow the egg mixture to drain from them. This will help the coating adhere and prevent it from falling off as you fry the crab cakes. Use one hand to handle the cakes when they are dry and the other when they are wet: you won't coat your fingers, and the cleanup will be faster.

North Side Scallops

4 tablespoons butter

¾ pound large sea scallops, patted dry

Black pepper

Salt

HEAT the butter until frothy in a hot skillet. Place the scallops in the butter and sear until the edges are crispy and slightly brown. Season the scallops lightly with pepper and salt. Turn them over and turn off the heat.

Presentation

(See the color photo illustrating the presentation of this dish.)

Chive oil (page 68)

Lovage leaves

POUR the chowder into 6 warm, wide, shallow soup bowls. Place a crab cake in the center of each, and add several seared scallops. Garnish with some chive oil and lovage leaves, and serve immediately.

WINE: Full-bodied dry white wine such as Chardonnay or Puligny-Montrachet.

Bacon Roast Loin of Pork with a Sweet Potato Pecan Wedge, Sage Peach Chutney, and Bourbon Gravy

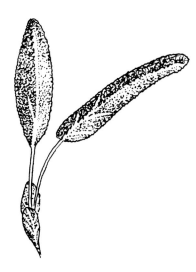

My dad is from the South. Some of his favorite flavors, including peach and sage, are combined in this dish. The roasting method is a perfect way to cook the two forms of pork.

6 SERVINGS

TIMING: Make the chutney and refrigerate overnight. ✳ Bake the sweet potato and refrigerate until thoroughly chilled, or overnight. ✳ Remove the chutney from the refrigerator to warm up. ✳ Prepare the pork and refrigerate for 60 minutes. ✳ Make the gravy. ✳ Roast the pork, and begin the presentation steps toward the end of the roasting time.

Sage Peach Chutney

½ cup sugar
¼ cup water
½ cup chopped onion
2 cups chopped unpeeled peaches

3 tablespoons red wine vinegar
1 teaspoon minced jalapeño
2 tablespoons thinly sliced sage

FOLLOWING the instructions on page 67, form a golden caramel with the sugar and water. Shock the caramel with the onion. Over medium heat, cook the onion for 5 minutes until it is translucent and half of the moisture has evaporated.

ADD the peaches, vinegar, and jalapeño. Stir gently just enough to combine. Reduce the heat to low, and simmer for 10 minutes, stirring occasionally. Add the sage and stir gently to combine. Remove the chutney from the heat and refrigerate overnight. Remove the chutney from the refrigerator in time to allow it to reach room temperature before serving.

CHEF'S HINTS

If the peaches are very ripe, they will break easily. Minimize the stirring so that they retain their shape. ✳ The best way to cut the sage leaves is to stack them on top of each other and then slice them as thin as you can. Chopping them will diminish their flavorful oils and the recipe will suffer. ✳ This recipe will yield about 3 cups. Store any excess in the refrigerator for several weeks.

Sweet Potato Pecan Wedge

1 large onion, minced (about 2 cups)
6 cloves garlic, minced
3 large sweet potatoes (about 3 pounds),
   cut into ¼-inch slices

Allspice pepper (page 66)
Salt
1 cup chopped pecans

Preheat the oven to 350°F. Line the bottom of a bread pan with wax paper, and lightly oil the sides.

Mix together the onion and garlic. Carefully layer the sweet potato on the bottom of the pan. Trim some pieces to line the edges evenly. Season the layer lightly with a little allspice pepper and salt. Sprinkle some of the onion mixture and some pecans on the sweet potato. Repeat these steps, gradually building up layers to a depth of about 4 inches. Finish with a layer of sweet potato. Press each layer firmly as the tart is built.

Tightly seal the pan with aluminum foil. Poke 2 small vent holes in the foil. Place the pan in the oven and bake until the sweet potato is tender, about 2 hours. Remove the foil and carefully press down on the sweet potato to compress it evenly.

Refrigerate the pan until thoroughly chilled, or overnight. Carefully insert a thin-bladed knife between the pan sides and the sweet potato to release the edges. Invert the pan onto a flat surface. Peel off the wax paper and carefully cut the loaf into wedge-shaped pieces. Reserve.

Variations: This method works well with almost any root vegetable, including turnips, potatoes, and beets. Sprinkle your favorite fresh herb or dried fruit in between the layers.

BACON ROAST LOIN OF PORK

3 pork tenderloins (about 1 pound each)
9 slices bacon, at room temperature

Black pepper
6 spaghetti noodles, raw

TRIM each tenderloin into 2 uniform pieces each about 5 to 6 ounces. Cut off the tapered end and remove the membrane on the other end. Each piece should be about 4 inches long. Reserve the trimmed off parts for another use.

CUT each bacon slice in half. Lay 3 half slices of bacon next to each other, slightly overlapping them along their long edges. Season the bacon liberally with black pepper. Let the bacon warm to room temperature so that it is flexible and easy to roll.

LAY 1 of the pork roasts sideways along the bottom edges of the bacon slices. Roll the pork in the bacon, stretching the bacon tightly. Thread the raw spaghetti through the overlapping ends of the bacon slices to secure them. Break off any overhanging ends of the spaghetti.

CHILL the pork roasts for 60 minutes. (Make the bourbon gravy.)

PREHEAT the oven to 400°F. Place the roasts on a roasting rack on a pan. Roast the pork until the bacon crisps and the meat cooks through, about 15 to 20 minutes (refer to the section on roasting meat on page 70). (Meanwhile, begin the presentation steps.) Remove the meat from the oven and let stand for 5 minutes in a warm place.

BOURBON GRAVY

6 slices bacon, chopped
½ cup water
1 cup chopped onion

3 cloves garlic, minced
½ cup bourbon
1 cup roast chicken broth (page 69)

PLACE the bacon and water in a small saucepan. Over medium heat, bring the mixture to a simmer and evaporate the water, stirring frequently. Continue cooking until the bacon is crisp. Add the onion and continue cooking until it begins to brown. Add the garlic and stir for a few minutes longer.

CHEF'S HINTS

The bacon should go around the meat only once and overlap just enough to be secured with the spaghetti. If the bacon is too long, trim it. ✴ The spaghetti will dissolve during the cooking process. ✴ Chilling the roasts well gives the bacon extra time to crisp before the heat penetrates to the center of the meat.

CHEF'S HINTS

By using the water when cooking the bacon, you speed up the rendering process without the risk of burning the bacon. ✴ The trimmings from the pork tenderloin could be browned and then simmered in the chicken broth before using it to make this gravy. ✴ If you don't have homemade chicken broth, use a high-quality, low-sodium canned variety.

ADD the bourbon and stir until all the browned bits on the bottom of the pot are loosened. Add the chicken broth. Bring the mixture to a simmer, reduce the heat, and simmer for 20 minutes.

PLACE the gravy in a blender and purée until very smooth. Strain through a fine mesh strainer and reserve. Taste the gravy before serving, and add a pinch or two of salt if needed.

PRESENTATION

Sage sprigs

TOWARD the end of the pork's roasting time, place the sweet potato wedges in the oven to warm them. When you remove the pork to let it stand for 5 minutes, turn off the oven and leave the wedges in it to continue reheating. A microwave will also work well for reheating the wedges.

REHEAT the bourbon gravy, if necessary. When the pork has been left standing for 5 minutes, place a sweet potato wedge on a warm dinner plate. Slice the pork across the grain with a sharp knife, being careful not to dislodge the bacon wrapping. Arrange the pork slices leaning against the longest edge of the sweet potato wedge.

POUR ¼ cup of the gravy over the pork and onto the plate. Place a spoonful of the chutney on top of the pork. Garnish with a sage sprig and serve immediately.

WINE: Medium- to full-bodied dry red wine such as Pinot Noir.

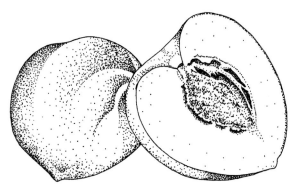

Campfire Style Rainbow Trout with Roast Potato Tarragon Salad and Pickled Rhubarb

The use of an improvised smoker in this trout recipe mimics the flavor given by a campfire. The tangy pickled rhubarb with its bright anise flavor complements the fish. Potato salad and a sprig of tarragon complete the presentation.

4 SERVINGS

TIMING: **Make the pickling syrup for the rhubarb, let stand 60 minutes, and strain. ✳ Make the potato salad. ✳ Smoke and sauté the trout. ✳ Reheat the syrup and cook the rhubarb toward the end of the trout cooking time.**

PICKLED RHUBARB

2 stalks rhubarb, cut into 3-inch pieces, then lengthwise into 4 sections

2 cups white wine

1 cup sugar

½ cup white wine vinegar

2 tablespoons ground star anise

SET the rhubarb aside; it will be cooked in the syrup just before the trout is served.

PLACE the wine, sugar, vinegar, and anise in a saucepan, bring to a simmer, and simmer for 5 minutes. Remove from the heat, and let the syrup stand for 60 minutes. Strain. (Make the salad and trout.)

AS the trout cooks, reheat the pickling syrup to a simmer, place the rhubarb pieces in the syrup, and cook until tender, about 2 minutes. Remove the rhubarb pieces from the syrup while they still retain their form (they will turn to mush in minutes).

Roast Potato Tarragon Salad

6 medium red skinned potatoes, cut into ½-inch dice (about 4 cups)
¼ cup extra virgin olive oil
1 teaspoon black pepper
1 teaspoon salt

1 cup sliced onion
3 cloves garlic, minced
2 tablespoons Dijon mustard
2 tablespoons red wine vinegar
2 tablespoons minced tarragon

PREHEAT the oven to 450°F.

TOSS the potato with 3 tablespoons of the oil, the pepper, and the salt, and place in a single layer on a baking sheet. Roast the potato, stirring occasionally, until crusty and cooked through, about 30 minutes.

MEANWHILE, sauté the onion in the remaining oil for 5 minutes. Add the garlic, and continue cooking until the onion is golden brown.

IN a large bowl, whisk together the mustard and vinegar. Add the roasted potato, onion, and tarragon. Toss the salad to combine all the ingredients. Set aside.

Campfire Style Rainbow Trout

2 cups small hardwood chips
8 rainbow trout fillets (about 3 to 4 ounces each)
2 eggs

¼ cup water
All-purpose flour
1 cup cornmeal
4 tablespoons butter

USING 2 metal pans of the same size, make a stovetop smoker. Fill the bottom of one pan with the wood chips. Place a lightly oiled cooling rack over the top of the pan. Invert the second pan on top of the rack creating a smoking chamber. Place the smoker directly over medium heat. When the chips begin to smoke after a few minutes, place the trout fillets skin down on the rack, leaving a space between them to help the smoke flow. You may have to smoke the fillets in several batches. Leave them in the chamber for 2 minutes. The fillets will have a slight pall and will smell smoky.

WHISK together the egg and water. Dredge each fillet alternately in flour, the egg mixture, and the cornmeal, shaking off any excess as you go.

IN a nonstick sauté pan, melt the butter over medium heat until it begins to foam. Place the coated fillets in the butter, and brown each side evenly, turning once. Cook until the fish is done, about 5 to 6 minutes in total.

PRESENTATION

(See the color photo illustrating the presentation of this dish.)

Tarragon sprigs

PLACE a mound of the potato salad in the center of a plate. Arrange 2 of the trout fillets on top of the potatoes. Arrange a few of the pickled rhubarb pieces on top of the fish. Garnish with a tarragon sprig.

WINE: Medium-bodied off-dry white wine such as Riesling or Gewürztraminer.

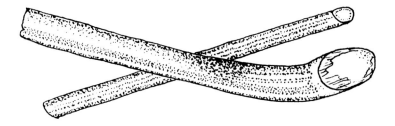

Roast Garlic Stuffed Breast of Chicken with Crisp Corn Pudding and Rosemary Vanilla Jus

Vanilla is often overlooked as a flavoring for savory dishes. Its affinity for rosemary is highlighted in this preparation. Although this recipe takes four or five hours to prepare, its flavors will reward you for your work.

4 SERVINGS

Timing: Roast the garlic for the chicken stuffing 60 minutes. ✳ Make the corn pudding and refrigerate. ✳ Bone the chicken breasts. ✳ Roast the chicken bones and scraps 60 minutes. ✳ Stuff the chicken breasts and refrigerate. ✳ Make the jus and simmer 2 hours. ✳ Strain the jus and reduce it while you coat the chicken breasts and bake them 30 to 40 minutes. ✳ Cut the pudding into pieces and sauté.

CHEF'S HINTS

Simmering the cobs in the milk draws an amazing amount of flavor from them. A skin will form on the bottom of the pot; ignore it. ✳ If you have a large nonstick saucepan, using it will speed cleanup. ✳ The pudding may also be served hot, directly from the pan, without the extra steps of cooling it down and then sautéing it.

CRISP CORN PUDDING

2 ears sweet corn
4 cups milk
4 tablespoons butter
½ cup minced onion

½ cup minced red pepper
½ teaspoon salt
1½ cups cornmeal

(Begin roasting the garlic for the chicken stuffing.) Cut the kernels off the ears of corn with a sharp knife and reserve. Cut each cob into several pieces, and place in a covered saucepan with the milk. Bring the milk to a boil, reduce it to a simmer, and continue simmering for 60 minutes. Strain the milk and reserve.

Melt the butter in a thick-bottomed saucepan. When it begins to foam and brown, add the reserved corn kernels. Stir the kernels in the butter until they begin to caramelize and brown. Add the onion and pepper, and cook a few minutes longer.

Measure the reserved milk. Add to it enough milk to equal 4 cups, and pour it into the corn mixture. Bring the milk to a simmer, add the salt, and, whisking continuously, slowly add the cornmeal in a steady stream until it is thoroughly combined. As the pudding thickens, begin stirring it with a spoon. Keep the mixture over low heat and stir it vigorously every few minutes. After 30 minutes, it will begin to pull away from the sides of the pot. When it pulls completely away it is done, after about 10 more minutes.

WORKING quickly, spread the hot pudding in a shallow baking dish and refrigerate for several hours. (Begin preparing the chicken breasts and the jus.)

CUT the cooled pudding into individual serving pieces using a biscuit cutter or knife. Just as the chicken finishes baking, crisp and reheat the pudding pieces in butter in a sauté pan, and serve.

ROAST GARLIC STUFFED BREAST OF CHICKEN

2 heads garlic, unpeeled
2 chickens (about 3½ pounds each)
½ cup snipped chives
¼ cup chive oil (page 68)
1 teaspoon salt
½ teaspoon black pepper

1 cup coarse dried bread crumbs
1 cup grated Parmesan cheese
2 eggs
¼ cup water
½ cup all-purpose flour

PREHEAT the oven to 350°F.

ROAST the garlic heads 60 minutes. (When done, turn the oven up to 400°F to preheat for the roasting of the chicken bones for the jus.) Allow the garlic to cool.

WHILE the pudding is cooking, rinse the chickens under cold running water. Remove the legs from the chickens, trim the meat off the legs, and reserve it for the mixture used to stuff the chicken breasts. Cut off the last 2 sections of each wing, leaving the third section attached to the carcass. Carefully remove the breasts from the chicken, leaving the remaining wing section attached to each breast. Remove the skin from the breasts and attached wing section by loosening it and tugging it firmly over the end of the wing bone. Save all the bones and scraps. (Begin roasting them for the jus.)

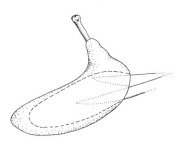

WITH a serrated knife cut off the root end of each garlic head and carefully squeeze out all of the roasted garlic. In a food processor, purée all of the reserved leg meat with the garlic, chives, chive oil, salt, and pepper until smooth. Place the purée in a large, heavy plastic bag and seal.

REMOVE the chicken tenderloins from the breasts and reserve. With a sharp, flexible boning knife, carefully cut a pocket into each breast (see drawing). Cut off 1 inch from a bottom corner of the plastic bag. Insert the cut corner of the bag deep into the chicken pocket, and squeeze out one-quarter of the stuffing into the breast.

To flatten the chicken tenderloins, put each between sheets of plastic wrap and roll gently with a bottle or rolling pin. Peel off the plastic, and insert the tenderloins just inside the pocket opening of the chicken breasts to function as a patch for the opening. Form each chicken breast into a smooth, even shape. Place in the refrigerator for 2 hours while the jus simmers.

When the jus has reached the reduction stage, preheat the oven to 350°F.

In a bowl, combine the bread crumbs and cheese. In another bowl, whisk together the eggs and water. Pat each chicken breast dry with a paper towel, then dredge it in the flour. Dip the chicken breast into the egg mixture, and then into the bread crumbs.

Place the breasts on a baking pan, and bake until cooked through, about 30 to 40 minutes. Let stand for 5 minutes before serving.

Rosemary Vanilla Jus

2 chicken carcasses
2 cups chopped carrot
2 cups chopped celery
2 cups chopped onion
8 cups water

2 cups Chardonnay
10 cloves garlic
1 teaspoon minced rosemary
4 vanilla beans

Place the carcasses, carrot, celery, onion, and any reserved chicken scraps in a roasting pan. Place the pan in the oven, and roast until the bones are golden brown, about 60 minutes. While they roast, return to stuffing the chicken breasts.

Remove the bones from the pan and place them in a large saucepan. Pour the water into the roasting pan, and stir to loosen all the encrusted scraps and drippings. When the pan is clean, pour the water into the pot with the bones. Add the wine and garlic. Bring the broth to a boil, reduce it to a simmer, cover, and continue cooking for 2 hours.

Strain the broth into another saucepan, and skim off any fat or froth that rises to the top. Place the saucepan over high heat, and bring the broth to a boil. Reduce the heat to medium, and begin reducing the broth. Carefully skim off any fat that rises to the top. When only about 3 cups remain, add the rosemary. Scrape the vanilla seeds from the vanilla pods, and add the

CHEF'S HINTS

While the chicken bones are roasting, it may be helpful occasionally to pour a small amount of water into the roasting pan. The water will dissolve any drippings and help keep the bottom of the pan from scorching. The drippings contribute an enormous amount of flavor to the broth, and so must not be allowed to burn. If necessary, to loosen the drippings easily at the end of the roasting, place the pan over direct heat and heat the water. ✳ Break the carcasses into smaller pieces so they won't protrude from the broth.

pods to the broth. When only 2 cups of broth remain, remove the pods. The total reduction time will be about 60 minutes.

PRESENTATION

(See the color photo illustrating the presentation of this dish.)

Rosemary sprigs   Chive oil (page 68)

PLACE a piece of pudding on a warm dinner plate. Carefully cut the chicken breast into 3 pieces and arrange them around the pudding. Pour ¼ cup of the broth onto each plate, garnish with a rosemary sprig and chive oil, and serve immediately.

WINE: Full-bodied dry white wine such as Chardonnay or Chassagne-Montrachet.

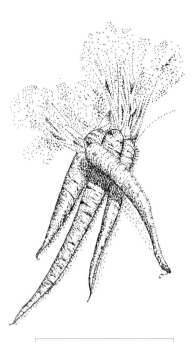

Slow Baked Salmon with Horseradish Salsa, Carrot Sauce, and a Salad of Pickled Carrots, Cucumber, and Watercress

Salmon is one of the most versatile fish available. Its unctuous texture is enhanced by this distinctive method of slowly cooking it until it is barely done. It will seem to melt in your mouth as the crisp watercress, pickled vegetables, and smooth carrot sauce accent its richness. The horseradish salsa provides a spicy twist.

4 SERVINGS

Timing: Make the pickled carrot and cucumber for the salad, and refrigerate 12 to 24 hours. ✳ Make the salsa and refrigerate overnight. ✳ Make the carrot sauce. ✳ Bake the salmon, reheat the sauce, and toss the salad.

CHEF'S HINTS

To cut the vegetables into long strips (julienne), a hand-operated machine called a mandoline is very useful. Its blades are adjustable for thin to thick slicing. ✳ Because the vegetables are pickled uncooked, they retain much of their crunch. ✳ Shaking the storage container keeps the oil and vinegar evenly distributed.

Salad of Pickled Carrots, Cucumber, and Watercress

Juice and zest of 1 lemon
1 tablespoon cider vinegar
1 tablespoon extra virgin olive oil
1 tablespoon honey
1 tablespoon snipped dill
½ teaspoon green Tabasco

½ teaspoon salt
½ cucumber, cut into match-stick size strips, seeds discarded (about ½ cup)
½ large carrot, cut into match-stick size strips (about ½ cup)
4 cups watercress, rinsed and dried

Place the lemon juice and zest, vinegar, oil, honey, dill, Tabasco, and salt in a small bowl. Whisk until thoroughly combined. Add the cucumber and carrot. Place the mixture in a small storage container and refrigerate it for 12 to 24 hours to allow the pickling process to take place. Shake the container occasionally.

To serve, pour the pickled carrot and cucumber and their pickling liquid into a large bowl, add the watercress, and toss to combine.

HORSERADISH SALSA

½ cup prepared horseradish
2 tablespoons extra virgin olive oil
Juice and zest of 1 lemon
2 cups chopped very ripe tomatoes

2 tablespoons snipped chives
½ teaspoon ground cinnamon
½ teaspoon ground cumin
½ teaspoon salt

SQUEEZE the horseradish to remove the excess water from it. Place the horseradish in a bowl with the oil and whisk together. Mince the lemon zest. Add the lemon juice and zest, tomato, chives, cinnamon, cumin, and salt to the horseradish mixture, and toss gently until just combined. Place the salsa in a storage container, and refrigerate overnight.

CARROT SAUCE

¼ cup extra virgin olive oil
2 cups diced carrot
1 cup water

2 cups carrot juice
½ teaspoon salt

IN a nonstick sauté pan, heat the oil over medium heat. Add the carrot, and sauté until golden brown and caramelized. Add the water, cover the pan, and simmer for 5 minutes, or until the water has completely evaporated.

PLACE the carrots in a blender with the carrot juice and salt, and purée until very smooth. Strain the sauce through a fine mesh strainer. Reserve.

WARM the sauce before serving.

CHEF'S HINTS

If you don't have a vegetable juicer, you can find carrot juice at many supermarkets or gourmet food stores. ✳ Caramelizing the carrots develops their flavor fully. Take the time to completely caramelize them, turning the heat down as you proceed. ✳ The added water allows the carrots to simmer, which dissolves their caramelized crust and ensures their doneness and a smooth sauce. ✳ To retain the freshness of its flavor and color, don't heat the sauce until just before serving.

SLOW BAKED SALMON

2 tablespoons extra virgin olive oil
½ teaspoon Bay Fortune seasoning
 (page 66)

4 salmon fillets, evenly thick (1½ to 2 inches,
 about 6 ounces each), skin removed
Salt

PREHEAT the oven to 250°F.

MIX together the oil and seasoning. Rub each of the salmon fillets with the oil mixture until evenly coated. Place the fillets on a baking pan in the center of the oven, and bake for 15 to 20 minutes until each fillet is heated through and just cooked. (Warm the carrot sauce and toss the salad as the salmon bakes.) Sprinkle with salt and serve immediately.

PRESENTATION

POUR ¼ cup of the sauce onto a warm plate. Add a pile of the watercress salad to the center of the plate. Nestle the salmon in the watercress, place a spoonful of the salsa on top of it, and serve immediately.

WINE: Medium-bodied dry white wine such as Sauvignon Blanc.

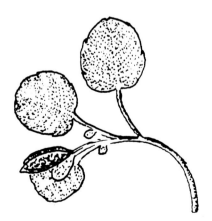

Rye Crusted Lamb Shank with Scotch Lentil Broth and Chanterelle Mushrooms

Lamb shanks are my favorite thing to cook. Although this method of preparing them takes about four hours, its simplicity is appealing. The assertive flavors of the Scotch and lentils go well with the lamb, while the chanterelles provide a delicate balance.

4 SERVINGS

TIMING: **Simmer the lamb shanks 2 to 2½ hours, let stand 1 hour, and remove from the braising liquid.** ✳ **Strain the braising liquid, and make the lentil broth.** ✳ **Coat the lamb shanks, and bake 20 to 25 minutes.** ✳ **Sauté the mushrooms.**

Rye Crusted Lamb Shank

1 cup extra virgin olive oil	3 tablespoons caraway seeds
4 lamb shanks (about 3 pounds in total)	1 teaspoon allspice pepper (page 66)
4 large stalks celery, diced (about 4 cups)	4 bay leaves
2 large carrots, diced (about 4 cups)	2 eggs
2 large onions, diced (about 4 cups)	¼ cup water
1 head garlic, peeled	2 cups rye flakes
4 cups Cabernet Sauvignon	1 teaspoon salt
4 cups roast chicken broth (page 69)	1 cup rye flour

IN a large, high-sided saucepan, heat the oil over medium heat until it just begins to smoke. Add the lamb shanks, and sear them on all sides until nicely browned. Turn the lamb shanks as needed, and be careful not to burn them.

REMOVE the lamb shanks and let them stand briefly on a cooling rack. Discard the remaining oil. Combine the celery, carrot, onion, and garlic, and place half of the vegetable mixture on the bottom of the saucepan. Arrange the shanks on top of the vegetables. Add the remaining vegetables, the wine, and the broth. Add 1 tablespoon of the caraway seeds, the allspice pepper, and the bay leaves. Bring the mixture to a boil. Reduce the heat until the broth is barely simmering, cover, and simmer for 2 hours.

CHECK the shanks for doneness by inserting a fork or thin-bladed knife into the meat. It should offer little resistance. If necessary, simmer for another 30 minutes.

CHEF'S HINTS

Ask your butcher for evenly shaped lamb shanks, and have them trimmed of the knuckle on the protruding bone. ✳ By using a high-sided pot, you avoid the splattering of the oil during the searing of the shanks. The large quantity of oil helps sear them evenly and quickly. ✳ At the Inn, we use lamb broth for this method; if you're ambitious, get some lamb bones and make some to use instead of the roast chicken broth. ✳ Don't allow the broth to boil during the braising.

CHEF'S HINT

As they cool in the broth, the lamb shanks absorb some of it. If they seem too loose for the coating process, refrigerate them until they become firm.

CHEF'S HINTS

By not adding the carrot until toward the end of the cooking, its color and texture are retained. The Scotch and sage are added at the end to preserve their flavors. ✳ The best way to cut the sage leaves is to stack them on top of each other, and slice them as thin as you can. Chopping them will diminish their flavorful oils and the recipe will suffer.

WHEN the shanks are done, turn off the heat and let them stand for 60 minutes in the braising liquid. Remove them with a slotted spoon, and place them on a pan or plate. Cover the shanks and let them cool to room temperature. Strain the braising liquid and reserve.

PREHEAT the oven to 350°F. (Begin preparing the lentil broth. While it is simmering, return to preparing the lamb shanks.)

WHISK together the eggs and water. Combine the rye flakes with the remaining caraway seeds and the salt. Coat the shanks by first dipping them in the rye flour, then in the egg mixture, and finally in the rye flake mixture.

PLACE the breaded lamb shanks on a baking sheet, and bake for 20 to 25 minutes until they are heated through.

SCOTCH LENTIL BROTH

1 cup minced shallots
2 tablespoons extra virgin olive oil
6 cloves garlic, minced
4 cups reserved lamb braising broth

1 cup French green lentils*
1 cup finely diced carrot
½ cup single malt Scotch
2 tablespoons thinly sliced sage leaves

French green lentils are the most flavorful variety and will retain their shape the longest.

IN a large saucepan, sauté the shallots in the oil until translucent. Add the garlic, and sauté for a few minutes more.

ADD the lamb broth and lentils. Bring the mixture to a simmer, cover, and simmer 25 minutes. Add the carrot and simmer 10 minutes more. Check the lentils for doneness; they should be cooked through but retain their shape and a hint of firmness. Cook them a few minutes more if necessary. When the lentils are done, add the Scotch and sage, and heat the mixture through.

Chanterelle Mushrooms

1 tablespoon butter
8 ounces whole chanterelle mushrooms,
   cleaned and dried

Black pepper
Salt

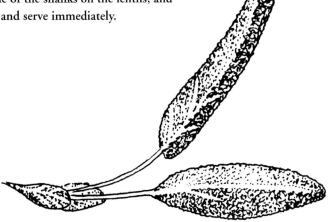

CHEF'S HINT

Rinse mushrooms if they are
particularly dirty, as our wild
chanterelles sometimes are.

WHEN the lamb shanks are almost heated through and the lentils are nearly done, melt the butter in a large nonstick sauté pan. When the butter begins to foam, add the chanterelles. Sauté them quickly, and season with freshly ground pepper and a few pinches of salt.

Presentation

(See the color photo illustrating the presentation of this dish.)

Sage sprigs

LADLE some of the lentils onto a warm serving plate. Place one of the shanks on the lentils, and add a spoonful of the chanterelles. Garnish with a sage sprig, and serve immediately.

WINE: Medium-bodied dry red wine such as Merlot.

Sautéed Lobster with Pea Pancakes, Pea Shoots, and Leeks in Cinnamon Basil Broth

This unique dish shows the remarkable affinity that lobster has for unusual flavors. The combination of basil and cinnamon increases the natural sweetness of the peas. In our kitchen garden, we grow cinnamon basil, a variety of basil with a wild spice flavor. It inspired this recipe. Have ready some fresh pea shoots for the presentation.

4 SERVINGS

TIMING: Cook the lobster, remove the meat, and refrigerate. ✳ Roast the lobster bodies and shells 30 minutes. ✳ Make the broth, and simmer 90 minutes. ✳ Make the pancake batter and refrigerate 60 minutes. ✳ Strain the broth, and reduce 30 minutes. ✳ Cook the pancakes. ✳ Cook the leeks.

CHEF'S HINTS

The lobster is cooked in the water only long enough to release the flesh from the shell. The claws are thicker and need slightly longer than the tails. ✳ Watch the tails as you sauté them. Their open "C" shape will begin to tighten as they heat; when the ends meet, the tail meat is done. The tails will spiral into a corkscrew shape if they overcook while glazing. Use high heat so the cooking and glazing progress together. ✳ For the presentation garnish, trim the heads so that they stand easily.

SAUTÉED LOBSTER

12 cups water	Large pot of ice
1 cup salt	1 tablespoon butter
4 live lobsters (about 1½ pounds each)	Juice and zest of 2 lemons

BRING the water and salt to a boil in a large, deep pot. Using a pair of gloves, remove the claws and knuckles from the live lobsters by twisting them off. Place the claws and knuckles in the water, and cook for precisely 2 minutes. Add the lobster tails still attached to the bodies. Cook for 1½ minutes. Remove all the lobster pieces, place them in a large pot of ice for a few minutes, and drain well.

SEPARATE the tails from the bodies by twisting them off. Carefully remove the meat from the knuckles, claws, and tails. Leave the claw meat whole, and cut the tails in half lengthwise. Set aside the knuckle meat for use in the pea pancakes. Reserve the bodies and shells for the cinnamon basil broth, and the heads for the presentation. Refrigerate the meat until ready for use. (Begin preparing the cinnamon basil broth.)

A few minutes before the presentation, in a large nonstick sauté pan heat the butter over high heat until it begins to froth. Add the claw meat and lobster tails, and sauté for several minutes. Mince the lemon zest. Add the lemon juice and zest and turn the lobster pieces, glazing them evenly as the liquid reduces and combines with the butter. Just before the presentation, pour any remaining liquid into the cinnamon basil broth. Serve immediately.

CINNAMON BASIL BROTH

Reserved lobster bodies and shells
¼ cup extra virgin olive oil
1 cup Chardonnay
1 teaspoon Bay Fortune seasoning (page 66)
2 cinnamon sticks
2 cups chopped carrot

2 cups chopped celery
2 cups chopped onion
1 head garlic, peeled
6 cups water
½ teaspoon ground cinnamon
2 cups basil leaves

PREHEAT the oven to 400°F.

TOSS the lobster bodies and shells in the oil and place in a roasting pan. Roast in the oven for 30 minutes, stirring occasionally. Remove the pan and place the contents in a large stock pot. Pour the wine into the pan and stir to dislodge any particles or drippings. Pour the wine and drippings into the stock pot. Add the Bay Fortune seasoning, cinnamon sticks, carrot, celery, onion, garlic, and water. Bring the broth to the boil, reduce the heat, and simmer for 90 minutes. Skim off any scum that rises to the top of the broth and discard. (Make the pancake batter.)

STRAIN the broth through a fine mesh strainer into a saucepan. Let the broth stand for a few minutes, and remove any scum or oil that floats to the top. Reduce the broth over medium heat with the ground cinnamon until 2 cups remain, about 30 minutes. Reserve. (Cook the pancakes.)

REHEAT the broth as the lobster tails are being sautéed. Purée the basil in a blender with some of the broth. Whisk the basil purée into the broth and serve.

Pea Pancakes

1 cup all-purpose flour	1 teaspoon chive oil (page 68)
1 teaspoon baking powder	2 cups fresh peas, shelled
½ teaspoon black pepper	2 tablespoons butter
½ teaspoon salt	⅔ cup cream cheese
¾ cup milk	¼ cup snipped chives
1 egg	Reserved lobster knuckle meat

Sift together the flour, baking powder, pepper, and salt. Whisk together the milk, egg, and chive oil. Place the peas in a food processor, and pulse briefly just enough to chop the peas into chunks. Don't process into a purée.

In a bowl, combine the peas and flour mixture. Add the egg mixture, and stir until the ingredients are just combined and still slightly lumpy. Refrigerate the batter for 60 minutes.

Heat the butter in a large nonstick skillet over a medium heat. Using about 2 tablespoons of batter for each pancake, spoon the batter onto the skillet to form 6 pancakes. Cook until the pancakes are golden brown and crispy around the edges, turn, and cook on the other side. Repeat with the remaining batter to form 6 more pancakes (for a total of 12 pancakes). Set aside to cool.

In a food processor, combine the cream cheese, chives, and reserved lobster knuckle meat. Process until a smooth paste is formed. Cut a slit along the edge of each pancake, and split it open slightly. Spread some of the paste inside with a butter knife. Repeat with all the pancakes. Set aside.

About 20 minutes before the presentation, preheat the oven to 350°F. Warm the pancakes as you cook the leeks.

Leeks

1 large leek
1 teaspoon butter
¼ cup Chardonnay

Black pepper
Salt

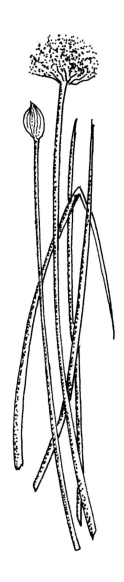

TRIM the bottom and dark green sections from the leek. Cut the remaining section into long thin pieces. Place the leek, butter, and wine in a small saucepan with a tight fitting lid. Briefly steam the leek over medium heat, just until tender. Season to taste with pepper and salt, and serve immediately.

Presentation

Lobster heads

Pea shoots

LADLE several ounces of the warm broth into each of 4 warm, large, shallow soup bowls. Stack 3 of the pancakes in each bowl, and place several pea shoots and some of the leeks between each layer. Arrange the lobster tails and claw meat around the pancakes. Garnish with the lobster heads and serve immediately.

WINE: Medium-bodied dry white wine such as Sauvignon Blanc or Fumé Blanc.

Pan Seared Skate Wing with Mint Tapenade and Roast Shallot Custard in Tomato, Chive, and Caper Water

Skate wing is often overlooked as a fish choice. The bold mint tapenade and vibrant tomato water accent its sweetness. The smooth custard provides a rich counterpoint to the other preparations in this dish.

4 SERVINGS

TIMING: Make the tapenade and refrigerate overnight. ✳ Make the tomato purée and drain 12 hours. ✳ Remove the tapenade from the refrigerator to warm. ✳ Finish preparing the tomato water and reserve. ✳ Bake the custard and let stand. ✳ Sear the skate wing and warm the tomato water.

CHEF'S HINTS

Don't use regular canned black olives for this recipe: their blandness is no match for the other ingredients. ✳ By briefly heating the garlic, some of its raw pungency is diminished. ✳ Stack the mint leaves on top of each other and slice as thinly as possible, in one direction only, with a very sharp knife. This will help preserve much of their essence, which would be lost if they were chopped. Use the most pungent mint available. At the Inn, our wild spearmint adds vibrancy to the tapenade.

MINT TAPENADE

2 tablespoons extra virgin olive oil
3 cloves garlic, minced
1 cup pitted Kalamata-style black olives
8 anchovies (about ½ cup), oil or brine
  squeezed out

Juice and zest of 1 lemon
½ cup minced red onion
½ cup thinly sliced mint leaves

BRIEFLY heat the oil and garlic in a small sauté pan. In a food processor, combine the olives, anchovies, lemon juice, and lemon zest. Add the garlic oil and process until a smooth paste is formed.

PLACE the olive paste in a bowl, and stir in the onion and mint. Refrigerate overnight. Allow the tapenade to warm to room temperature before serving.

TOMATO, CHIVE, AND CAPER WATER

6 large very ripe tomatoes
½ cup snipped chives
¼ cup capers

½ teaspoon Tabasco
Salt

PURÉE the tomatoes in a blender. Place the tomato purée in at least 6 layers of moistened cheesecloth, and gather the ends of the cheesecloth together to form a bag. Hang it over a bowl for 12 hours, or until the purée stops draining.

PLACE the tomato water, chives, capers, and Tabasco in a small saucepan. Taste, and carefully add salt until the tomato water is lightly seasoned. Reserve.

JUST before the presentation, warm the tomato water until it is just heated through.

ROAST SHALLOT CUSTARD

6 shallots, finely minced
¼ cup extra virgin olive oil
1 cup heavy cream
½ cup Chardonnay

2 whole eggs
1 egg yolk
½ teaspoon salt
¼ teaspoon white pepper

PREHEAT the oven to 350°F. Lightly oil 4 (5- or 6-ounce) ramekins. Cut a small circle of wax paper and fit it into the bottom of each ramekin.

SAUTÉ the shallots in the oil until golden brown. Add ½ cup of the cream and the wine. Reduce the liquid until only ½ cup remains.

BRING a kettle of water to the boil.

IN a bowl, whisk together the eggs and egg yolk. Add the remaining cream, the salt, the pepper, and the shallot mixture. Whisk together completely. Divide the custard mixture evenly between the prepared ramekins.

PLACE the ramekins in a shallow baking pan on the lower shelf of the oven. Pour in the hot water until it reaches two-thirds of the way up the sides of the ramekins. Bake until the custards are set, about 40 minutes. Carefully remove the pan from the oven, cover loosely with foil, and let the ramekins stand in the water for a few minutes until the skate wing is ready to be served.

CHEF'S HINTS

For this method, be sure to use the highest quality, vine-ripened juicy tomatoes available. ✳ At the Inn, we use a cotton pillowcase to drain the tomatoes. By moistening the cloth first, the fibers swell and prevent any of the tomato solids from leaking through when the purée is first added. ✳ To preserve its amazing freshness, don't heat the tomato water until just before you are ready to serve it.

CHEF'S HINTS

Mince the shallots very fine or they will float to the top of the custard. ✳ By adding the water to the pan when it is already in the oven, you avoid splashing any water into the unbaked custards.

CHEF'S HINTS

Ask your fishmonger to clean
and trim the skate wing of all
skin and sinew. ✳ Although
the cooking time depends on
the thickness of the fillets,
skate cooks very fast.

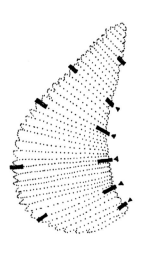

PAN SEARED SKATE WING

4 skate wing fillets (5 to 7 ounces each), trimmed and cleaned	Salt
Black pepper	½ cup superfine flour*
	¼ cup extra virgin olive oil

Superfine flour yields a very crisp coating and is also used as a gravy thickener. It is sometimes called instant flour and is available in supermarkets or specialty food stores.

THOROUGHLY dry the skate wing fillets with paper towels. Make a series of small cuts along the edges, with the grain (see drawing). This will help keep the flesh from curling as it cooks.

SEASON each fillet with pepper and salt, then dust each thoroughly with the flour. Heat the oil in a large nonstick sauté pan over high heat. Add the fillets, and cook until browned, about 3 to 5 minutes on each side. Serve immediately.

PRESENTATION

Chive oil (page 68)	Mint sprigs

DIVIDE the tomato water evenly between 4 large, shallow, warm soup plates. Gently run a thin-bladed knife around the edge of each custard, releasing it from the ramekin. Invert each ramekin onto a plate, and transfer the custards to the bowls of tomato water. Drape the skate wing over the custard. Place a spoonful of the mint tapenade on top of the fish. Spoon some drops of chive oil into the tomato water, garnish with a mint sprig, and serve immediately.

WINE: Full-bodied white wine such as Chardonnay or Côtes du Rhone.

Last Courses

The finishing touch: a dessert nears completion.

Dessert is a time of celebration, a time for indulgence. Often the most memorable part of a meal for many guests, dessert offers the opportunity for total reckless enjoyment and undisciplined dining. Calorie counting eases as cream and butter become more prominent. Chefs and diners throw culinary caution to the wind, and embark on fanciful flights of sweet ecstasy. Team Cuisine strives to have meals end with a flourish.

Despite what seems to be evidence to the contrary, many of the guidelines that influence my culinary sensibilities throughout the planning and preparation of earlier courses are retained at dessert. Although I relax my hesitance to use cream and butter, the finish of my guests' dining experience at the Inn is as important as the beginning. For every preparation on the dessert menu, the role that each element plays in that preparation is carefully considered. Flavors are complementary, textures are varied, and presentation must be relevant. The cooking methods, if anything, become more precise: pastry, for example, is an art that requires extreme discipline.

I often interject savory elements into the last course of a meal. Many of the Inn's guests are not interested in totally sweet preparations and are more comfortable with cheese, nuts, and other savory ingredients. Some of the following recipes reflect this preference.

10:22 pm: "Sixteen plate!" announces the chef. With a final, concerted effort, Team Cuisine is assembling the last few entrée orders of the evening. Seconds tick by as the motivated cooks finish the presentations. The chef quickly summons servers, and, as the steaming hot plates disappear, he checks the expeditor's board. "Board's clear. Get the towels!" Everyone but the dessert cook makes a dash for the nearby beach. Within minutes the staff are in and out of the water, dressed in their uniforms, and back in the kitchen to start the breakdown. Their absence was timed perfectly! Guests enjoy their meals contentedly as the kitchen swirls with cleaning activity. Tomorrow awaits. Team Cuisine and the kitchen will be ready.

After the glamour comes the reality: cleanup!

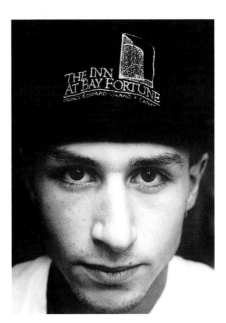

First cook Norman Aitken ready for action.

Cashew Rhubarb Tart with Rosemary Ice Cream and Raspberry Port Sauce

I describe this preparation as a grown-up dessert. The flavors are familiar, but are combined in a unique manner that distinguishes this dessert. The rosemary ice cream is made in an ice-cream maker, available at department and specialty cooking stores. For a special presentation, dry rosemary sprigs in the oven overnight, and, just before you serve this dessert, set them on fire, blow out the flame, and crown the tart with a smoking rosemary sprig.

6 TO 8 SERVINGS

TIMING: Make the ice cream and freeze. ✳ Make the sauce and refrigerate. ✳ Prepare the tart dough and refrigerate 20 minutes. ✳ Stew the rhubarb and set aside. ✳ Form the tart shell and bake 20 minutes. ✳ Fill the tart shell and finish baking.

ROSEMARY ICE CREAM

3 cups heavy cream

½ cup clover honey

2 tablespoons minced rosemary

6 egg yolks

¼ teaspoon salt

PLACE the cream, honey, and rosemary in a saucepan, and bring the mixture to a simmer. Remove it from the heat, and let it stand 2 hours.

WHISK together the egg yolk and salt with 1 cup of the cream mixture. Bring the remaining cream mixture to a simmer over medium heat. Slowly whisk in the egg yolk mixture. Continue heating and stirring until the cream mixture begins to thicken and will coat the back of a spoon. Do not allow the mixture to boil. Strain the mixture through a fine mesh strainer and place in the refrigerator until cool, about 60 minutes.

FREEZE in an ice-cream maker following the manufacturer's instructions.

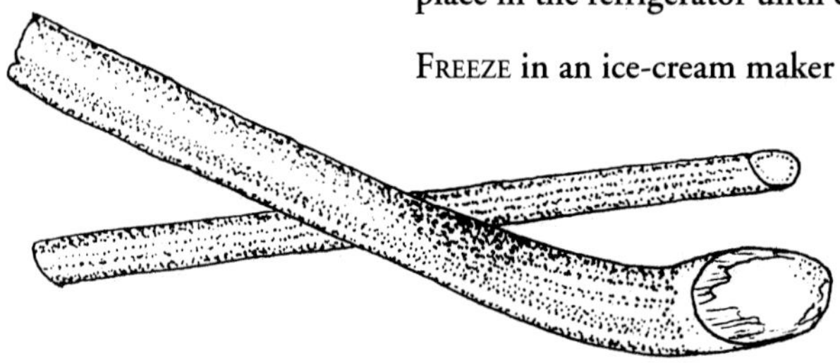

RASPBERRY PORT SAUCE

1 cup Port   ½ cup sugar
1 cup raspberries

COMBINE the wine, raspberries, and sugar in a small saucepan. Bring the mixture to a simmer, and cook for 2 minutes.

PURÉE the sauce thoroughly in a blender, and strain through a fine mesh strainer into a storage container. Refrigerate until chilled, about 60 minutes.

CASHEW RHUBARB TART

¾ cup plus ⅔ cup all-purpose flour   8 cups diced rhubarb
1⅔ cups chopped cashews   1 cup Cabernet Sauvignon
1 cup granulated sugar   1 teaspoon minced rosemary
2 teaspoons grated lemon zest   ¼ teaspoon water
¼ teaspoon salt   ⅔ cup packed light brown sugar
¼ pound frozen butter, cut into 8 pieces ⅓ pound butter, melted (⅔ cup)
2 egg yolks

PROCESS ¾ cup of the flour, 1 cup of the cashews, ⅓ cup of the granulated sugar, the lemon zest, and the salt in a food processor briefly until evenly combined. Add the frozen butter, and process until the mixture resembles coarse crumbs, about 30 to 40 seconds. Add 1 of the egg yolks, and process a few more seconds until the dough begins to form a ball.

LIGHTLY flour your hands and remove the dough, patting it into an even, cohesive ball. Refrigerate the dough about 20 minutes until it stiffens and is easy to work with.

MEANWHILE, place the remaining granulated sugar, rhubarb, wine, and rosemary in a saucepan. Bring the rhubarb mixture to a simmer over medium heat, and stew 30 minutes, stirring occasionally as the water gradually evaporates. When the rhubarb mixture is very thick, remove it from the heat, and set aside until the tart shell is baked.

CHEF'S HINTS

Decorative edges don't work with this pastry; instead, fashion a crisp, even edge. ✳ Toward the end of the 30 minutes, gently stir the stewing rhubarb more frequently as it will begin to stick. Try not to break up the fragile rhubarb pieces. Make sure that the rhubarb mixture is very thick before removing it from the heat. ✳ At the Inn, we use 4-inch individual tart pans, available at specialty cooking stores, for this dessert.

PREHEAT the oven to 400°F.

PLACE the dough in either 1 (10-inch) removable-bottomed tart pan, or 6 (4-inch) or
8 (3½-inch) removable bottomed tart pans. Pat the dough evenly into the bottom and sides,
and prick thoroughly with a fork. Bake the shell until it is golden brown, about 15 minutes.
Whisk together the remaining egg yolk and water, and brush the egg mixture onto the inside
of the shell with a pastry brush. Continue baking 1 minute longer to set the glaze.

WHILE the tart shell is baking, process the remaining cashews and flour with the brown sugar
and melted butter briefly in the food processor until the cashew mixture resembles coarse
crumbs. Turn the oven down to 350°F. Add the stewed rhubarb to the baked tart shell and
sprinkle the cashew mixture evenly over the top. Bake for a further 20 to 30 minutes until the
topping browns. Remove the tart from the oven, and let it cool to room temperature before
serving, about 60 minutes.

PRESENTATION

Rosemary sprigs

IF a large tart was made, remove it from the tart pan and cut into slices. If individual tarts were
made, cut them in half and place the pieces on the plate so that they are offset from each other,
forming an "S."

PLACE a scoop of the ice cream beside the single slice of tart, or at the intersection of the 2 slices
of the individual tarts. Pour several tablespoons of the sauce across the ice cream and tart onto
the plate. Garnish with a rosemary sprig.

A Time for Chocolate: Molten Bittersweet Chocolate Cake with Cookie Clock Hands, Allspice Pepper Sautéed Bananas, and Rum Froth

These clocklike little cakes with their cookie clock hands are the all-time favorite dessert at the Inn. The presentation is always a show-stopper, but it requires timing. You will need an icing kit, available in supermarkets or specialty food stores.

6 SERVING-SIZED CAKES

TIMING: Prepare the chocolate cake batter and refrigerate for at least 2 hours, or up to 2 days. ✳ Make the batter for the cookie clock hands and refrigerate 2 hours ✳ Form the cookie clock hands and bake. ✳ Several hours ahead, decorate 6 plates and refrigerate them. ✳ Bake the cakes. While they are baking, sauté the bananas and make the froth.

Molten Bittersweet Chocolate Cake

8 ounces bittersweet chocolate (8 squares)
¼ pound butter (½ cup)
½ teaspoon ground allspice
5 eggs, separated
¼ cup sugar

2 tablespoons molasses
2 teaspoons vanilla
1 cup all-purpose flour
2 tablespoons cocoa powder

PLACE the chocolate, butter, and allspice in a large stainless steel bowl. Place the bowl over a pot of simmering water. As the chocolate begins to melt, stir it until it is smooth. When about one-quarter of the unmelted chocolate remains, remove the bowl from the heat and continue stirring until all the chocolate is melted.

IN a separate bowl, whisk together the egg yolk, sugar, molasses, and vanilla. Add the yolk mixture to the chocolate mixture and stir until combined. Add the flour and cocoa powder, and stir to combine.

IN a separate bowl, whip the egg white with a mixer on high speed until a stiff meringue forms. Add one-third of the meringue to the chocolate mixture, and stir until completely combined. Using a rubber spatula, gently fold in the remaining meringue, and continue folding until completely combined. Place the batter in a storage container and refrigerate until thoroughly chilled, about 2 hours, or even up to 2 days. (Make the cookie clock hands and decorate the plates before baking the cakes.)

CHEF'S HINT

These cakes are intentionally underbaked so that when they are served their centers are hot and gooey. By chilling the batter, the amount of time that the center of each cake remains cool is extended. The trick is to cook the batter long enough so that the outside sets and is strong enough to hold the center firmly. If you should accidentally overbake the centers, you'll be left with a very moist, flavorful chocolate cake that is eminently servable.

PREHEAT the oven to 400°F. Lightly butter and flour 6 (6-ounce) baking molds. Divide the chilled batter between the molds. Place the molds on a baking sheet and bake for exactly 12 minutes. (Meanwhile, sauté the bananas and make the rum froth.) Let the cakes stand for 2 minutes before serving.

Cookie Clock Hands

4 tablespoons butter
4 tablespoons molasses
⅔ cup sugar

⅔ cup all-purpose flour
3 egg whites

PLACE the butter, molasses, and sugar in a food processor. Combine until a smooth paste is formed. Add the flour and egg white, and continue processing until thoroughly combined. Process the mixture for 2 minutes longer. Place the batter in a storage container and refrigerate until thoroughly chilled, about 2 hours.

USING a stiff piece of plastic and a very sharp utility knife, cut out templates for a large and a small clock hand. The opening in the templates should be about ¼ inch wide so that the cookie clock hands are not too fragile. Make a template about 4 inches long for the large hand, and about 2½ inches long for the small hand.

PREHEAT the oven to 350°F. Place the templates on a nonstick baking sheet. Use a flexible palette knife to spread an even layer of the batter into the openings of the 2 templates. Lift the templates and repeat until 12 hands are formed. Bake them until they are set and golden brown, about 7 to 8 minutes. Let the cookie clock hands cool, then gently remove them from the baking sheet and reserve.

Allspice Pepper Sautéed Bananas

3 ripe bananas, peeled
2 tablespoons butter

2 teaspoons allspice pepper (page 66)
3 tablespoons sugar

SEPARATE each of the bananas into 6 equal pieces using the technique described in the chef's hint. Heat the butter in a large nonstick sauté pan. When the butter begins to foam, add the

CHEF'S HINTS

Don't make the template openings too narrow, or the cookie clock hands will be too thin and delicate. ✳ If you don't have a nonstick baking sheet, lightly oil a regular baking sheet. ✳ Make a few more hands then you will need; one or two always break.

CHEF'S HINT

To separate a peeled banana into 6 pieces, cut the banana in half across the middle. Gently drive your little finger into the exposed cross section of a banana half — it will separate perfectly into 3 pieces.

banana pieces and the allspice pepper. Sauté the bananas briefly, then sprinkle the sugar onto them.

GENTLY toss the bananas until they are well coated with the butter glaze. Set aside while you prepare the rum froth.

RUM FROTH

6 egg yolks

½ cup confectioners' sugar

½ cup dark spiced rum*

½ cup water

Dark spiced rum is a full flavored rum with spicy nuances. It is widely available.

PLACE the egg yolk and sugar in a stainless steel bowl and place the bowl over, not in, a pot of simmering water. In a separate bowl, mix together the rum and water. Whisk the egg mixture until it becomes foamy, and then gradually add the rum mixture, whisking continuously.

CONTINUE whisking vigorously until the mixture doubles in volume. It will thicken and become creamy. Serve immediately.

PRESENTATION

(See the color photo illustrating the presentation of this dish.)

Chocolate icing

BEFORE you begin to make the cakes, use an icing piping kit to pipe a stylized clock face around the rim of 6 plates. Refrigerate the plates to set the icing.

SCOOP some rum froth onto each plate. Arrange 3 of the banana pieces in the center of the froth. Unmold the cakes, and set a cake on top of the bananas on each plate.

CAREFULLY poke the base ends of the clock hands into the cakes to resemble a clock. At the Inn, we always make sure that the clock hands indicate the time when the dessert arrives at the guest's table. Serve immediately.

CHEF'S HINT

Direct heat can scorch the rum froth. Make sure that the pot is broad enough so that heat doesn't rise up the outside of it to the bowl. Don't overwhisk the froth, or it will break — the egg yolk will overcook and separate from the rum.

Roasted Carrot Cake with Cream Cheese Sauce, Carrot Ice, and Minted Carrots in Riesling Syrup

The lowly carrot has amazing potential. This recipe takes advantage of the many forms that a carrot can take and highlights some sophisticated flavors that can accompany it. The pan roasting of the carrot will yield an intensely flavored carrot jam that makes this carrot cake particularly moist and flavorful.

8 SERVINGS

> TIMING: Make the carrot ice and freeze overnight. ✳ Make the carrots in syrup and refrigerate overnight. ✳ Make the cream cheese sauce and refrigerate. ✳ Bake the carrot cakes.

CHEF'S HINT

The egg white helps keep the ice from becoming so hard that it is unusable. It replaces some of the sugar that would otherwise be needed to make the ice soft. The resulting ice has a pleasing, rather than overwhelming, sweetness.

CARROT ICE

2 cups carrot juice
¾ cup sugar

½ teaspoon salt
1 egg white

IN a small saucepan, heat 1 cup of the carrot juice, the sugar, and the salt until the sugar dissolves. Remove from the heat and add the remaining juice. Gently whisk in the egg white until it is just combined. Place the mixture in a storage container, and freeze overnight.

MINTED CARROTS IN RIESLING SYRUP

2 cups sugar
2 cups Riesling
1 teaspoon salt

16 baby carrots, peeled, greens reserved
for garnish
½ cup finely sliced mint

COMBINE the sugar, the wine, and salt in a saucepan, bring to a boil, and dissolve the sugar. Add the carrots, reduce the heat, and simmer for 5 minutes. Add the mint. Place in a storage container and refrigerate overnight.

BEFORE serving, remove the carrots from the syrup and let them drain briefly. Reserve the syrup.

CREAM CHEESE SAUCE

2 cups heavy cream
1 teaspoon ground nutmeg
½ teaspoon salt

½ cup honey
3 egg yolks
½ cup cream cheese, softened

PLACE the cream, nutmeg, and salt in a small saucepan, and heat until the cream begins to simmer. In a separate bowl, whisk together the honey and egg yolk. Add ½ cup of the hot cream to the egg mixture, and whisk to combine. Whisking continuously, slowly add the egg mixture to the simmering cream. Continue stirring the cream over medium heat as it cooks and begins to thicken.

AFTER several minutes of cooking, the cream should coat the back of a spoon. Turn off the heat. Add the cream cheese and continue stirring until it melts and forms a smooth sauce. Pour the sauce into a container, and refrigerate until chilled.

CHEF'S HINT

Adding some of the hot cream to the egg mixture tempers it so that the eggs will not scramble instantly when added to the hot cream. Once the egg yolk is incorporated, the cream will thicken in just a few minutes. As the sauce cools, it will thicken more.

ROASTED CARROT CAKE

¼ pound butter (½ cup)
3 cups chopped carrot
4 tablespoons honey
1½ cups all-purpose flour
1 cup brown sugar
1½ teaspoons baking soda
1 teaspoon baking powder

1 teaspoon ground cinnamon
½ teaspoon ground allspice
½ teaspoon ground cloves
½ teaspoon salt
3 eggs
2 teaspoons vanilla
1 cup finely grated carrot

IN a large saucepan, heat the butter until it begins to foam. Add the chopped carrot and pan roast, stirring frequently until it caramelizes and darkens. Lower the heat gradually as the carrot cooks to prevent burning. The carrot will shrivel and intensify in color. After 45 minutes, add the honey and simmer 5 minutes more. Place the carrot mixture in a food processor and process until thoroughly puréed. Set aside.

CHEF'S HINTS

If you don't have individual ramekins or baking molds, a large muffin pan will work. ✳ The ramekins may be filled with batter in advance and baked when needed. The cakes can be left at room temperature for several hours and warmed in the oven before serving.

PREHEAT the oven to 350°F. Lightly oil and flour 8 (6-ounce) ramekins. Cut a small disc of wax paper or parchment paper and insert it into the bottom of each ramekin.

SIFT together the flour, sugar, baking soda, baking powder, cinnamon, allspice, cloves, and salt. In a large bowl, whisk together the egg and vanilla. Add the carrot purée, and combine. Add the flour mixture and the grated carrot to the egg mixture. Stir the batter until thoroughly combined.

DIVIDE the batter evenly between the prepared ramekins. Bake until a toothpick inserted in the center comes out clean, about 30 minutes. The cakes will be firm to the touch. Let the cakes stand for 10 minutes, then loosen them from the ramekins with a thin-bladed knife. Invert the cakes onto serving plates and serve warm.

PRESENTATION

(See the color photo illustrating the presentation of this dish.)

8 mint sprigs

POUR ¼ cup of the sauce onto 8 chilled dessert plates. Cut off the top of each cake. Place a cake bottom in the center of the sauce. Add a scoop of the carrot ice, and perch the cake top on it. Arrange the minted carrots and a mint sprig decoratively on each plate. Spoon some of the reserved Riesling syrup around the cream cheese sauce. Garnish with the reserved carrot greens.

Star Anise, Chocolate, and Pistachio Tart with Sambuca and Mint Soaked Grapefruit

This dessert highlights the exotic, licorice-like star anise. Its aromatic, spicy flavor combines with the chocolate to make this one of the most distinctive desserts at the Inn. The grapefruit's citrus edge rounds out the richness of the mousse.

6 SERVINGS

TIMING: Prepare the grapefruit peel and dry overnight. ✳ Make the tart dough and refrigerate 60 minutes. ✳ Bake the tart shells and let them cool. ✳ Make the tart filling, fill the tart shells, and refrigerate 1 to 2 hours. ✳ Finish preparing the grapefruit and let stand 60 minutes as the tarts cool.

Sambuca and Mint Soaked Grapefruit

2 grapefruits

2 cups sugar

2 cups water

½ cup sambuca

2 tablespoons finely sliced mint

CHEF'S HINTS

Blanching the peel in a sugar syrup removes some of its bitterness. ✳ A gas oven turned off will be just warm enough from its pilot light to dry the peel overnight. ✳ Try not to break the fruit sections as you remove their membranes. Use the membranes as a guide for the knife blade.

CUT off the peel of each grapefruit in large pieces. Reserve the grapefruit in the refrigerator. Remove the white pith from the peel, and dice enough of the peel into small, uniform pieces to fill ¼ cup.

PREHEAT the oven to 150°F.

BRING 1 cup of the sugar and 1 cup of the water to a simmer. Add the diced grapefruit peel and simmer 5 minutes in the syrup. Strain, and discard the first syrup. Repeat these steps with the remaining sugar and water. Place the peel on a piece of wax paper on a baking pan, and dry overnight in the warm oven.

(MAKE the tarts.) With a small, sharp knife, carefully section the grapefruit, cutting between the membranes and discarding the seeds. Collect any juice that squeezes out. Place the sections in a small bowl. Add the dried peel, any reserved juice, the sambuca, and the mint. Toss the grapefruit mixture lightly just to combine, and let it stand 60 minutes.

CHEF'S HINTS

When making pastry, working with very cold ingredients keeps the butter from melting into the flour. Many pastry chefs refrigerate all of the pastry ingredients and the tools used to make it. By remaining separate in very small pieces, the butter makes the pastry tender and flaky. Don't overmix the butter into the flour, or the butter will melt. Stop the food processor when the ingredients are completely combined but not smooth; the butter will remain in tiny lumps. ✳ If you don't have individual tart molds, use a large tart pan. ✳ The dough should be no thicker than 1/4 inch. Trim any overhanging dough from the tart pans, and form a decorative edge. ✳ The beans weigh down the pastry while it bakes, keeping it from becoming puffy.

STAR ANISE, CHOCOLATE, AND PISTACHIO TART

THE TART PASTRY

1¼ cups all-purpose flour

5 ounces butter, frozen (⅝ cup)

2 tablespoons sugar

¼ teaspoon salt

1 egg yolk

3 tablespoons ice water

PLACE the flour, butter, sugar, and salt in a food processor. Process until completely combined and the mixture resembles lumpy sand.

IN a bowl, mix together the egg yolk and ice water. Add the egg mixture to the flour mixture and process briefly, just until the dough is moistened and begins to clump together.

KNEAD the dough on a lightly floured surface just until the dough is smooth. Wrap it in plastic wrap, and refrigerate 60 minutes.

PREHEAT the oven to 325°F.

DIVIDE the dough into 6 equal pieces. Roll each piece out on a lightly floured surface, and fit the dough into 6 (4-ounce) tart pans. Prick the dough evenly on the sides and bottom with a fork. Place a small piece of foil in each shell, and weigh it down with a few spoonfuls of dried beans. Bake the shells 15 minutes. Take them out of the oven, remove the beans and foil, and let the shells cool.

THE TART FILLING

1½ cups heavy cream

2 tablespoons ground star anise

2 tablespoons molasses

1 cup shelled pistachios

12 ounces bittersweet chocolate
  (12 squares), chopped

¼ pound butter (½ cup)

PREHEAT the oven to 350°F.

IN a small saucepan, bring the cream, anise, and molasses to a simmer. Remove the cream mixture from the heat, and let it stand 30 minutes.

PLACE the pistachios on a baking sheet and roast them 10 minutes. Cool the pistachios, then chop them coarsely in a food processor.

PLACE the chocolate and butter in a large bowl. Return the cream mixture to the heat and bring to a simmer. Strain the cream mixture through a fine mesh strainer into the chocolate mixture, and let it stand 5 minutes. Whisk the chocolate mixture until smoothly combined.

DIVIDE the chocolate mixture evenly between the pre-baked tart shells, pouring it carefully into each. Sprinkle the top of each tart with chopped pistachios. Refrigerate the tarts 1 to 2 hours until firm.

CHEF'S HINT

Heating the cream mixture helps to infuse it with the flavor of the star anise.

PRESENTATION

Mint sprigs

CUT the chilled tarts in half. Place one half on a chilled dessert plate. Lean the other half on the first half. Place a spoonful of the grapefruit compote in between the pieces, and garnish with a mint sprig.

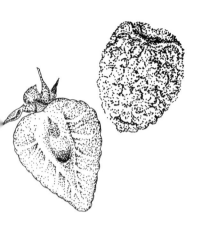

Seasonal Berry Compote in a Crisp Cookie Cup with Chardonnay Ice and Lemonade Sauce

At the Inn we eagerly await the start of berry season every summer. As the various berry harvests overlap, the different berries contribute to the spontaneity of this dish. The fat-free sauce is very easy to make, and will complement many desserts. The presentation is simple, but loaded with crisp flavors that accentuate the freshness of the berries.

6 SERVINGS

TIMING: Make the cookie batter and refrigerate overnight. ✳ Bake the cookies, let them cool a few minutes, and form them into cups. ✳ Make the ice and freeze 4 to 6 hours. ✳ Make the sauce and refrigerate about 2 hours. ✳ Make the berry compote.

Crisp Cookie Cup

⅓ cup corn syrup   4 tablespoons butter
⅓ cup sugar   ½ cup all-purpose flour

PLACE the corn syrup, sugar, and butter, in a small pot over medium heat. Stir until the butter melts and the ingredients are combined. Add the flour, remove from the heat, and continue stirring until a smooth batter is formed. Refrigerate the batter overnight.

PREHEAT the oven to 350°F. Lightly oil a baking sheet.

FORM small balls with 1 tablespoon of the chilled cookie batter. Place the balls 4 inches apart on the baking sheet. Bake until the batter spreads out and turns a deep golden brown, about 10 minutes.

LET the cookies cool for a few minutes until they become pliable. Working quickly, invert each cookie onto a small cup or other form and press the sides of the cookie down to form a cup shape. If the cookies have cooled too much, they will be harder to form without breaking; return them to the oven briefly if necessary. Let the cookie cups cool completely, and remove them from the forms. Store the cookie cups in an airtight container until ready for use.

CHEF'S HINTS

Chilling the batter makes it easier to work with, but it will bake easily when warm. ✳ Don't make the balls too big: they will spread dramatically. ✳ Make sure that the cookies are evenly browned before removing them from the oven. If the cookies brown unevenly in your oven, remove the ones that are ready and form them. Bake the remaining cookies until golden brown. The lighter the color, the weaker the cookie cup and the more likely it will be to stick to your teeth as you eat it. ✳ The upper surface of these cookies is more textured than the bottom surface; flipping the cookie onto the form shows off the texture.

CHARDONNAY ICE

1½ cups Chardonnay   ½ cup sugar

POUR ½ cup of the wine into a saucepan and add the sugar. Heat the wine mixture over medium heat, just until the sugar dissolves. Turn off the heat, and add the remaining wine.

POUR the wine syrup into a shallow pan. Cover it, and place it in the freezer until the syrup begins to freeze. Stir the syrup with a fork, breaking up the ice into chunks. Continue freezing and stirring occasionally, until the syrup is completely frozen, about 4 to 6 hours.

LEMONADE SAUCE

Juice and zest of 6 lemons   2 cups water
3 Granny Smith apples, peeled, cored, and   ½ cup sugar
  chopped (about 4 cups)   ¼ teaspoon salt

COMBINE the lemon juice and zest, apple, water, sugar, and salt in a saucepan, and bring the mixture to a simmer. Cover, and continue simmering until the apples are soft, about 10 minutes.

POUR the lemon mixture into a blender, and purée it until very smooth. Strain it through a fine mesh strainer. Pour the purée into a storage container, and refrigerate until chilled, about 2 hours.

SEASONAL BERRY COMPOTE

4 cups very ripe mixed berries   ½ cup confectioners' sugar

TOSS the berries gently in the sugar until they are just coated. Let the compote stand for 10 minutes before serving.

CHEF'S HINT

Sugar will not freeze, nor will alcohol. These two factors keep the Chardonnay syrup from freezing rock hard as water would.

CHEF'S HINTS

Granny Smith apples will not oxidize and turn brown, thus discoloring the sauce. ✴ The fragrant lemon flavor of the sauce is entirely dependent on the lemon zest. ✴ Taste the sauce before you add the salt. You'll see that salt is very important for sweet preparations, as well as savory ones.

CHEF'S HINT

As the sugared berries stand, the sugar draws some of the moisture out of the berries and forms a syrup.

PRESENTATION

POUR ¼ cup of the lemonade sauce onto each of 6 chilled, large dessert plates. Place a cookie cup on each plate. Divide the berry compote evenly between the cookie cups, reserving some of the syrup. Place a scoop of the Chardonnay ice on the berries. Drizzle some of the berry syrup onto the lemonade sauce on each plate.

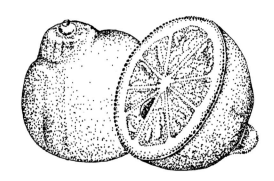

WALNUT CRUSTED BLUE CHEESE CAKE WITH PORT SAUCE AND PEAR MINT CHUTNEY

Savoring blue cheese is one of my favorite ways to end a meal. Walnuts, pears, and Port combine to give this dessert a sweet and savory flourish.

6 SERVINGS

TIMING: **Make the chutney and refrigerate overnight.** ✳ **Make the sauce.** ✳ **Make the cakes.** ✳ **Remove the chutney from the refrigerator to warm while the cakes bake.**

PEAR MINT CHUTNEY

½ cup sugar

¼ cup water

1 medium onion, diced (about 1 cup)

2 tablespoons red wine vinegar

1 teaspoon salt

1 teaspoon Tabasco

1 teaspoon vanilla

½ teaspoon ground nutmeg

1 large pear, diced (about 2 cups)

¼ cup thinly sliced mint leaves

CHEF'S HINTS

Chutney is defined by a balance of various taste sensations. ✳ Be sure that the pear is very ripe. To avoid breaking the pear pieces, don't stir the chutney when the pear is added.

FOLLOWING the instructions on page 67, form a caramel with the sugar and water, then shock the caramel with the onion. Return to the heat, and stir the onion as it begins to extrude moisture. Simmer over medium heat 10 minutes to reduce the liquid.

ADD the vinegar, salt, Tabasco, vanilla, and nutmeg. Bring the onion mixture to a simmer, and add the pear. Continue heating just until the pear is heated through, about 1 minute. Remove the chutney from the heat, add the mint, and stir just to combine. Refrigerate overnight. Let the chutney reach room temperature before serving it.

PORT SAUCE

1 large pear, diced (about 2 cups)

1 cup Port

2 tablespoons butter

IN a small saucepan, bring the pear, wine, and butter to a simmer, and simmer 1 minute. Process the pear mixture in a blender until thoroughly puréed. Set aside.

CHEF'S HINTS

Make sure that the crust is an even thickness when you form it. The cheese cake will bond with the crust, and, if the crust is too thick in some areas, it will be left behind when the ramekins are inverted. Be especially attentive to the area where the bottom and sides meet. ✳ Don't overbeat the batter; leave it somewhat chunky. ✳ Use a small spoon to add the batter to the crusts, and be careful not to knock loose the sides of the crusts. ✳ The cakes are best served at room temperature. If necessary, they may be baked ahead, refrigerated, and reheated briefly in a microwave.

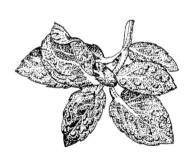

WALNUT CRUSTED BLUE CHEESE CAKE

1 cup walnuts
1 cup large-flake rolled oats
4 tablespoons butter, frozen

½ cup cream cheese, at room temperature
3 eggs
¾ pound blue cheese, at room temperature

PREHEAT the oven to 350°F. On a baking sheet, toast the walnuts until they darken, about 15 minutes. Remove and let cool.

IN a food processor, combine the walnuts and oats until they are ground into fine crumbs. Add the butter, cut it into pieces, and process until a ball is formed, about 30 seconds.

PLACE 3 tablespoons of the nut mixture in each of 6 (4-ounce) ceramic ramekins. Using your fingers, form an even crust, patting the nut mixture into place on the bottom and sides of the ramekins. Bake the ramekins 15 minutes. Remove them from the oven, and firmly pat the hot crust with the back of a spoon, flattening it against the ramekins' sides and bottoms. Let stand as you prepare the batter.

TURN the oven down to 325°F. Bring a kettle of water to the boil.

IN a food processor, purée the cream cheese with 1 of the eggs until smooth. Add the remaining eggs and process briefly. Add the blue cheese and process until the blue cheese is combined but still slightly chunky. Divide the batter evenly between the ramekins.

PLACE the filled ramekins in a pan, and place on a low shelf of the oven. Fill the pan with enough hot water to come two-thirds of the way up the sides of the ramekins. Bake 40 minutes.

REMOVE the pan and let the cheese cakes cool in the hot water 30 minutes. Remove them from the water, and let cool 60 minutes. Carefully invert each ramekin onto your hand. Discard any crust scraps. Serve.

PRESENTATION

Mint sprigs

POUR ¼ cup of the Port sauce onto each of 6 plates. Place a cheese cake in the middle of the sauce, and a spoonful of the chutney on top of the cake. Garnish with a mint sprig.

Hot Hot Chocolate with White Chocolate Whipped Cream

This chocolate sprinkled hot chocolate is a dessert all by itself. Its name refers to the pleasing edge that the cayenne, allspice, and cloves give the chocolate. A hint of heat with chocolate can be a great combination.

4 SERVINGS

White Chocolate Whipped Cream

4 ounces white chocolate (4 squares)   ½ cup heavy cream, at room temperature

CHOP the chocolate and place it in a stainless steel bowl over simmering water. Stir occasionally until the chocolate has melted completely. Remove from the heat, and let the chocolate cool to room temperature.

WHIP the cream until it is frothy. While continuing to whip the cream, slowly add the melted chocolate. Whip the cream until it becomes stiff. Refrigerate the whipped cream while you prepare the hot chocolate.

Hot Hot Chocolate

12 ounces bittersweet chocolate (12 squares)   1 teaspoon ground cinnamon
1½ cups heavy cream   ½ teaspoon cayenne
1½ cups milk   ½ teaspoon ground allspice
4 tablespoons molasses   ¼ teaspoon ground cloves
2 teaspoons vanilla

CHOP the chocolate into small pieces and place it in a bowl. In a small saucepan, heat the cream to a simmer and pour it over the chocolate. Let the cream and chocolate stand 5 minutes.

IN the same saucepan, heat the milk, molasses, vanilla, cinnamon, cayenne, allspice, and cloves just until the milk comes to a simmer. Stir the cream and chocolate together until thoroughly combined. Add the chocolate mixture to the milk mixture, and stir to combine thoroughly. Serve immediately.

CHEF'S HINTS

By adding the chocolate at the last minute, the possibility of scorching it is reduced. ✳ Use a large pot so that if the milk foams, it doesn't make a mess.

Presentation

Chocolate shavings

Pour the hot hot chocolate into 4 festive mugs. Add a large dollop of the white chocolate whipped cream, and sprinkle some chocolate shavings on top.

INDEX

METRIC EQUIVALENTS

GENERAL FORMULA FOR METRIC CONVERSION

Ounces to grams: multiply ounce figure by 28.35

Pounds to grams: multiply pound figure by 453.59

Pounds to kilograms: multiply pound figure by 0.45

Ounces to milliliters: multiply ounce figure by 30

Cups to liters: multiply cup figure by 0.24

Fahrenheit to Celsius: subtract 32 from the Fahrenheit
 figure, multiply by 5, then divide by 9

Inches to centimeters: multiply inch figure by 2.54

VOLUME

1 teaspoon = 5 milliliters

1 tablespoon = 15 milliliters

¼ cup = 60 milliliters

⅓ cup = 80 milliliters

½ cup = 120 milliliters

⅔ cup = 160 milliliters

1 cup = 230 milliliters

WEIGHT

1 ounce = 28 grams

1 pound = 454 grams

OVEN TEMPERATURES

300°F = 150°C

325°F = 165°C

350°F = 175°C

375°F = 190°C

400°F = 200°C

425°F = 220°C

450°F = 230°C

475°F = 245°C

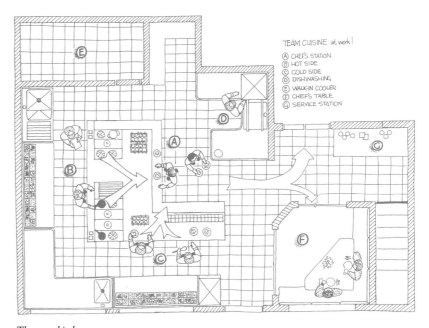

TEAM CUISINE at work!
- (A) CHEF'S STATION
- (B) HOT SIDE
- (C) COLD SIDE
- (D) DISHWASHING
- (E) WALK-IN COOLER
- (F) CHEF'S TABLE
- (G) SERVICE STATION

The open kitchen.

About the Inn

The Inn at Bay Fortune nestles on the eastern end of Canada's Prince Edward Island. The Inn's 20 hectares (46 acres) face Bay Fortune as it opens out to the Northumberland Strait. The Inn is located 12 kilometers (8 miles) from the Magdalen Islands ferry in Souris, and 70 kilometers (45 miles) from the island's capital, Charlottetown, on Scenic Kings Byway, Route 310.

Contact The Inn at Bay Fortune at:

Bay Fortune
Souris, RR #4
Prince Edward Island, Canada C0A 2B0
TEL: (902) 687-3745 (summer season mid-May to mid-October)
 or (860) 296-1348 (off season)
FAX: (902) 687-3540
E-MAIL: innatbayft@auracom.com
INTERNET: www.innatbayfortune.com
INNKEEPER: David Wilmer

Credits

All illustrations by Michael Smith. (The illustrations are available in color as a limited edition print series suitable for framing. Please call the Inn for details.)
Photos on pages 10, 12, 13, 15, 16, 19, 20, 21, 25, 27, 28, 30, 32, 34, 52, 63, 64, 65, 67, 69, 77, 94, 95, 130, and 131 by Jack Leclair.
Photos on pages 9, 17, 23, 33, 51, 61, 71, 75, 93, and 129 from the Artville Food in Detail Photography collection.
Photos (color) on insert pages by Julian Beverage.
Kitchen equipment courtesy of Paderno (www.paderno.com).